Summers Under
The Tamarind Tree

SUMAYYA USMANI

Summers Under
The Tamarind Tree

RECIPES & MEMORIES FROM PAKISTAN

SUMAYYA USMANI

FOOD PHOTOGRAPHY BY JOANNA YEE

FRANCES
LINCOLN

Quarto is the authority on a wide range of topics.

Quarto educates, entertains and enriches the lives of our readers—enthusiasts and lovers of hands-on living.

www.quartoknows.com

Frances Lincoln Limited
74–77 White Lion Street
London N1 9PF

Summers Under the Tamarind Tree
Copyright © Frances Lincoln 2016
Text copyright © Sumayya Usmani 2016

Food photography copyright © Joanna Yee

Design: Sarah Allberrey
Commissioning editor: Zena Alkayat

Travel photography copyright © Shaukat
Niazi p2, p6, p10tl, p13, p14, p28, p36, p52.
© epa/Corbis: Rashid Iqbal p72; Omer Saleem p108.
© Corbis: Roger Wood p154. © AFP/Getty Images:
A. Majeed/Stringer p75; Asif Hassan p92; Nadeem
Khawar p124, p180. © Getty Images: Sanal Thomas/
Em Eye p8; Metin Aktas/Anadolu Agency p10tr;
Bashir Osman p10b.

A catalogue record for this book is available from the British Library

ISBN 978-0-7112-3678-3

Printed and bound in China

9 8 7 6 5 4 3 2

This book is for my mother, grandmothers and daughter – the women who have always inspired me – and for my homeland, which is full of passion, promise and authentic flavour.

Contents

Summers under the tamarind tree

Memories of my childhood come flooding back when I conjure up an image of a lofty tamarind tree. This arbor stood regally in my grandmother's garden and offered both sanctuary and solitude, and I spent so much of my youth under its branches and lounging on the cool earth above its deep roots.

The fruit it bore was enveloped in a crusty brown shell, yielding a rather ugly, pulpy flesh, which at first bite would send shivers down my spine. The tamarind certainly wasn't the most attractive fruit in that garden, but its sour flavour was always the most inviting to me as a child, and despite endless warnings of side effects (ranging from a sore throat to the early blossoming of womanhood!) I'd still venture to pick another fruit, or even chew on the tree's little bittersweet leaves. Then I'd curl up underneath its boughs and read my book knowing that the tamarind tree's intoxicating tang would soon tempt me again.

As a child I couldn't fully appreciate the power of tamarind to balance taste sensations and its Midas touch when it comes to flavour enhancement. My first inkling of its magic abilities came while eating lashings of tamarind chutney piled on to chaat (a spicy chickpea snack) at one of Pakistan's many roadside stalls. There was also my favourite summer drink – a spiced tamarind nectar which brought calm to hot summer days.

It's the umami quality of tamarind that has grown to inspire much of my Pakistani cooking, and it finds its way into my recipes. When I moved to the UK, I was struck by the fact that despite a large Pakistani diaspora, our cuisine never found its individual voice. My patriotic spirit and passion for the food I grew up cooking and eating sowed the seeds for this book. I hope that the flavour of my heritage comes through in each recipe I share.

Pakistan: the spirit, the passion, the flavour

When people think of Pakistan, they probably picture a simple land plagued by troubles. But having grown up in Karachi, to me Pakistan means a peaceful, happy childhood filled with exciting scents, sounds and, most importantly, flavours. Food is the spirit of Pakistani people and it's something that has been many thousands of years in the making. —

To understand the food of Pakistan you need to visualise a country of diverse land, climate and people. You need only look to its borders to understand the varied influences the country is blessed with. In the north, there's China, Tibet, the rugged Hindu Kush mountains and the foothills of the Himalayas (from which the fertile River Indus flows like an artery through Punjab and down to the Arabian Sea). And Pakistan is flanked by Afghanistan and Iran on the west, and India on the east. In the south, the country meets the arid dry deserts of Tharparkar and the silver sandy beaches of the Arabian Sea, which gently kisses my home city of Karachi.

This mixed geography means a wealth of natural resources, from coconut trees and dates to rosewood and juniper trees, as well as rice, wheat and sugarcane. But perhaps the biggest impact on Pakistan's cuisine is the myriad historical invasions, settlements and migrations. It's a country that has over 20 different languages and dialects, and it's enriched by a confluence of people and traditions.

Relatively young, Pakistan formed in 1947. It was previously part of the British Empire and was created amid much political turmoil as a home for Indian Muslims distinct to India. Before it was Pakistan, this region of the subcontinent played home to many overlapping civilisations and empires, from the Greeks led by Alexander the Great, via reigning Rajput dynasties and on to the Arab, Mughal and Sikh Empires. The ancient influences of these settlers can still be felt, as well as that of the immigrants who arrived in the newly formed Pakistan from India and beyond, bringing their own sophisticated cuisines with them. It means that each province of Pakistan not only boasts its own geographical characteristics, but also disparate ethnic communities, religions, traditions and culinary styles too.

The eastern province of Punjab, for example, has always had abundant farmland, and the food here is rich and hearty, often spicy and aromatic, and distinctively infused with cardamom, saffron and cloves. Beyond the fields, Punjab's capital Lahore is an architecturally stunning masterpiece: majestic buildings such as the Lahore Fort, Badshahi Mosque (pictured on the following page) and Shalimar Gardens are the legacy left by the Mughals. This is also where you'll find famous enclaves dedicated to street food, all alive with smoky barbecues and sizzling meat dishes.

In the southeastern province of Sindh and Arab imprints can be felt, and it's from here that Islam found its way into the subcontinent. Its coastline also saw it become a gateway to the spice trade in the 1600s and the food in this region is characterised by brilliantly flavoured saltwater and freshwater seafood.

Balochistan in the southwest is dramatically different: the land is arid and barren, the summers are harsh and hot, and the winters severe. In the simple, meat-heavy, often barbecued dishes, you might spot Afghan, Turkish and Mongol influences – though little or no spice is used, and sometimes meats are dusted only with salt and pepper.

Nothing is simple about the make-up of Pakistan – but it's easy to see how its history has helped create what we now call contemporary Pakistani cuisine. What unites all in Pakistan is an attitude toward food: Pakistanis love to eat and to feed others. Hospitality is key. Food always takes centre stage, be it an everyday meal or times of celebration and even of sorrow. And while Pakistan is a nation of many faiths, its Muslim culture and cuisine that has the greatest impact on the way we eat.

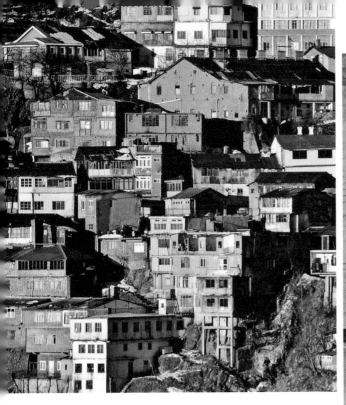

It determines how our meat is slaughtered, inspires the prayer people say before mealtimes and teaches us to share food with guests and be generous to the poor.

There's a sense of togetherness that defines the Pakistani meal, whether at home or at work – it is a time to talk, reflect, share and laugh. Come lunch, businesses close so employees can eat together, all seated around a 'dastarkhan' (a dining spread on the floor), regardless of age, background or belief. And while street stalls in Pakistan are full of enticing food, eating at home as a family is a fundamental part of everyday life.

A typical Pakistani meal is pretty simple. Always using seasonal produce, it includes bread, rice and a pickle and comprises ingredients with properties that are either 'thanda' (cold) or 'garam' (hot), with the balance of flavours essential. Though our cuisine is meat-heavy, most meals will also include humble cooked lentils and vegetables. Special occasions such as an Eid feast or a wedding dinner are never complete without an array of barbecued meats, slow-cooked curries and rich aromatic biryanis all adorned with saffron, pistachios, mint, rose or screwpine water. Fish is also enjoyed in both coastal and riverside towns – spices and masalas for seafood are fragrant, featuring lots of fresh herbs, cumin and carom seeds.

I hope the stories and recipes in *Summers Under the Tamarind Tree* bring to life my country's food and culture, as well as my own eating and cooking experiences growing up as a first-generation Pakistani born to Muslim Indian immigrants. And most of all I hope that it inspires you to see the country in a whole new light.

From top left My Nani and Nana (maternal grandparents) in 1942;
My mother with me as a baby; Me lounging on one of the deck of the
Ocean Endurance, one of the merchant navy ships my father captained

Childhood tales
Growing up in the kitchen

Almost all of my memories of growing up involve food, and just like Pakistani produce, each is seasonal.

I remember helping my Nani (maternal grandmother) tend to her garden in spring, looking after her fragrant motia (jasmine) flowers and picking bhindi (okra) that was full of earthy freshness. By summer, I'd take shelter from the sun under mango trees before climbing them to reach the fruit. As summer ended, balmy monsoon showers brought the chance to lie on the flat roof of my family home, breathing in the smell of damp earth and eating hot pakoras. And mild southern winters meant curling up with my mother under soft woollen blankets while sipping hot cardamom chai. I grew up with a sense of pride in being Pakistani – and the belief that flavour was paramount.

My most treasured memories are of the hours spent in my family kitchen, unknowingly learning cooking styles and recipes steeped in Muslim heritage from the women in my family. I would watch my grandmothers, mother and aunts in the kitchen, and I learned through smelling and tasting food (rather than from written down recipes) how to make authentic family dishes. We celebrate recipes handed down through the generations, and at home everything is cooked by 'andaza' (estimation).

Think of andaza as sensory cooking: learning to taste, breathing in aromas, to find the recipe right for your taste buds. I was taught never to be a slave to a recipe, so feel free to make these your own by experimenting with the flavours of Pakistan that I share. This is the foundation of my cooking style instilled from a young age, and it is one I follow to this day.

From top My Nani (maternal grandmother) in front of her house where I spent so many days growing up; Me and my mother at a food market on one of our European travels; My father working in naval headquarters as aide-de-camp to the navy chief

From top left Me in my pink gharara at an Eid lunch; Me dressed up ready for Eid with my Nani in her wonderful garden; My early interest in kitchen equipment in my first home in Karachi; In the centre of the photo is my Dadi (paternal grandmother) flanked by my Dada (paternal grandfather) and my parents on the left, and Anwar Khala on the right

Cooking methods
Pakistani techniques explained

The cornerstone of Pakistani cuisine is its cooking methods. Incorporating these into your kitchen skills will help create the true taste of Pakistan. I picked up many of these methods from the cooks in my family while growing up, and in time I've realised that they contribute a vast amount to the character of Pakistani food. I think my grandmothers would be proud to know I can pass on these treasures to my daughter one day…

1. Bhunai (removing moisture and enhancing flavour)

This is by far the most important method in my family repertoire. My mother, who is both my fiercest critic and my greatest inspiration, to this day thinks that my food is often 'bhuno-ed' too lazily! It's a technique unique to the subcontinent and based on ancient Mughal cooking. It takes patience and perseverance to master bhunai; however, the results elevate a mediocre dish into a spectacular one. The basic concept of bhunai (when cooking meat, poultry or vegetables) is to remove all the moisture from the cooking ingredients (such as onions, garlic and tomatoes, as well as the meat and veg itself). This process gives the cooking oil (which was initially used to fry the ingredients, and which is infused with spices at the beginning of the cooking) a chance to permeate into these ingredients for a richer flavour. For a meat or chicken in a sauce (or curry), wait until the meat is tender and then turn the heat up to high and fry the meat and sauce vigorously, using a spoon to move the meat around and avoid it sticking. If there isn't any oil left in the pan, add about 2 tablespoons of vegetable or sunflower oil. This can be drained off later. Cook until all the moisture leaves the pan – this can take about 15–20 minutes. You'll know the bhunai has been successful when you notice the following: the colour of the sauce becomes dark; the oil separates from the spices and rises to the surface of the sauce; the aroma of the dish becomes more fragrant.

2. Tenderising by boiling

Many meat and daal (lentil) dishes make use of the tenderising-by-boiling method. This involves combining spices together with the main ingredient (meat, vegetables or daal) and then slow-cooking them together with water or yogurt. This creates a stock-like liquid for dishes such as railway curry (p79) and aloo gosht (p83).

3. Tarka or bhagar (tempering)

Pouring infused oil on to dishes after they've been cooked is called tarka or bhagar. This can also be done at the beginning of a dish to flavour the base oil. Oil or ghee is heated until it's spitting hot, then ingredients are added to flavour the oil in order of cooking time: so, dry spices are added first (such as cumin and mustard seeds), followed by slow-to-cook ingredients (such as garlic and onions). When using only dry spices, begin with seeds like cumin, followed by spices such as dried chillies and finally curry leaves – only cook the leaves for 2-3 seconds. The key is not to burn the ingredients in the oil as it will make the dish taste bitter and burnt. As soon as the hot oil is infused with the spices and ingredients, pour it on to your prepared dish and cover it immediately with a lid. This ensures that all the oil's flavour goes deep into the dish and doesn't escape.

4. Dum (steaming)

Dum is the method that brings dishes like biryani to life. Dum means cooking a dish in its own steam, and is a technique that originated in Persia where food was cooked in a 'degchi' (large pot) and sealed with dough. This would then traditionally have been buried in hot sands or under coals to let the dish gently cook in its own steam and juices, infusing it with delicate flavour. Many Pakistani meat dishes are cooked under dum giving the meat a chance to slow-cook and tenderise. To do this, you can cook your meat dish in a lidded saucepan on the hob (over a low heat) or using a lidded dish (such as a casserole dish) in the oven.

Dum is used for cooking biryanis and pulaos, and the method involves cooked or par-boiled rice, which is drained and then cooked through using steam. For example, to use a dum method for biryani, layer rice that has been par-boiled for 3-4 minutes over a completely cooked, thick meat or chicken curry. When layered, cover the saucepan firmly with a piece of foil turning it over the lip of the saucepan – this ensures that no steam escapes the pan while the biryani is cooking. Then place a tight-fitting lid on top. Cook for 12–15 minutes on a very low heat (use a heat diffuser under the pan if you can) to complete the cooking. In some traditional biryani recipes, the dum process actually cooks through raw meat and raw rice together, but this takes years of practice to perfect!

5. Dhuni (smoking)

This is my favourite cooking method – it's basically infusing meat or vegetables with coal smoke. Dhuni is typical in the subcontinent and many recipes call for it at the end of the cooking process. It is also a great alternative when you are not able to barbecue as it adds that sweet coal flavour to a dish. See bihari kebabs (p76) and follow this step-by-step guide:

- Place the kebabs, mince or vegetables in a saucepan with a tight-fitting lid. Make a small gap in the middle of the pan and place either a small piece of bread, a balled-up bit of foil, or a piece of garlic or onion skin.
- Light a small round of quick-light coal. Using tongs, place the hot burning coal on to the bread/foil/skin.
- Pour over 1 tablespoon vegetable oil or ghee. Smoke will begin to rise almost immediately. Cover at once.
- Leave until the coal stops smoking – this should take about 10–15 minutes.
- Remove the coal and the foil/bread/skin and discard. The dish should now be smoked and ready to serve.

6. Galavat (tenderising)

Much of the meat in Pakistan is tough, mainly mutton and chicken which is usually tenderised when marinated using natural tenderisers such as raw papaya, kalmi shora (saltpetre, as in hunter beef, p90), or kachri powder (a wild cucumber variety that is dried and powdered). Almost all kebabs are tenderised using one of these ingredients mixed in the marinade, and the result is a soft kebab with an almost melt-in-the-mouth texture.

7. Homemade ghee

This is not really a cooking method, but a home essential – nothing quite compares to homemade ghee. My mother always made it using a stash of fresh cream that had been skimmed off buffalo milk. As it simmered on the hob for hours, it released rather intense aromas – a certain cocktail of melted butter and astringent hay. When it turned amber and smelt of butterscotch, it was ready. Making ghee from cream is an exercise in patience, so I usually make it using unsalted butter, as below…

This recipe takes about 30–40 minutes, and makes 250ml/9fl oz/1 cup liquid ghee. If you want it to be particularly butterscotchy, cook for the full 40 minutes and it should go a very dark amber colour.

- Heat 250g/9oz/1 cup unsalted butter in a saucepan over a low heat until it's melted and scum rises to the top – anything between 25–40 minutes. Skim occasionally, until all scum stops rising.
- Allow to cool slightly before pouring through a sieve into a sterilised, heatproof storage jar with a lid. Cool completely before closing the lid. Keep at room temperature and use in 10–15 days, or keeps up to 3 weeks in the fridge.

8. Homemade tamarind pulp and sauce

The ready-made tamarind pastes you can buy in supermarkets aren't anywhere near as good or authentic as a homemade version. The store-bought stuff can be bitter, and lacks the subtlety tamarind adds to a dish. Make the pulp yourself from dried tamarind blocks which can be bought in South Asian shops and online. You can then use it as a base for spiced tamarind sauce (see below), or added directly to a dish to give it a sweet sour flavour.

This recipe makes about 300ml/10 fl oz/1¼ cups tamarind pulp.

- Add 220g/8oz/1 cup dried tamarind (with seeds and fibres) in a ceramic or glass bowl (not metal). Add about 300ml/10 fl oz/1¼ cups hot boiling water and leave it to soak for 30 minutes or overnight.
- Using your hands, squeeze the pulp until seeds and fibres come apart and you're left with a thick pulp.
- Pour into a fine mesh sieve over a clean bowl. Squeeze further to release a thick, smooth pulp and then discard all the fibres and seeds. (Scrape paste from bottom of the sieve into the bowl, as a lot will accumulate there.)
- Store chilled up to 2-3 weeks in a covered container, or freeze in an ice-cube tray up to 3 months.
- **To make tamarind sauce**: To 300ml/10 fl oz/1¼ tamarind pulp, add 1 tsp dry roasted cumin, ½ tsp kalanamak (black salt), ¼ tsp black pepper, ½ tsp chilli powder, 50g/1¾oz brown sugar and 2 tbsp water.
- Soak 20g/¾oz stoned, soft dates in hot water for 30 minutes. Drain. Then combine with the tamarind mix.
- Blitz the mixture in a blender until thick and combined. Pass through a medium sieve (not too fine).
- Pour into a glass jar. It keeps in the fridge for up to 5 days. Dilute further with water if you like.

A note on spice

Over the years of teaching cookery, I've learned that people's apprehension of using spice comes from being nervous about gauging the quantities to add, as well as which stage to add it. Spice shouldn't be viewed as a daunting enemy – let it be your companion in the creation of flavour, learn to play with it, use it to complement your food. Nothing is lost if you begin by adding a little spice, and build the quantity up. It's also worth noting that spice isn't synonymous with heat – it's usually the addition of chilli that creates the heat. In Pakistani cooking, chilli is added at a cook's discretion and many recipes include little or no chillies during cooking – instead, much of the heat comes from adding fresh chopped green chillies at the end, which can easily be omitted.

The art of using spices in Pakistani food doesn't come from a set blend, but rather from personal creativity and confidence. And I believe anyone can find their own personal flavour. Use my recipes and spice measurements as your basic guide and experiment to create your own Pakistani flavour. But remember, the real key to cooking Pakistani dishes is perfect seasoning, as no amount of spice will ever rise to the occasion without a balanced amount of salt.

Growing up, I was taught that the two ingredients to spend money on are the best quality Pakistani basmati rice and only the best whole spices, never ground, unless freshly home-ground. This rule will give you that authentic Pakistani flavour. Buying the bigger bags of good quality spices in bulk, and with long expiry dates, from ethnic stores is the more cost and quality effective way of shopping for spices. Many different spices are used in this book; however, my basic go-to spices are below, and buying a small supply of these will enable most of the dishes in the book to be cooked. Store what you use daily in South Asian spice tins for accessibility, and store the remaining quantities in airtight jars.

- Whole cumin seeds
- Whole coriander seeds·
- Green cardamom
- Black cardamom
- Cinnamon
- Cloves
- Black peppercorns
- Star anise
- Long, dried red chillies

Masala blends
Traditional family recipes

Each family has its own subtly different masala blends which are passed down through the generations. They're what make each Pakistani cook's dishes unique. These are my taste of home…

Mummy's garam masala ('daal dust')

My mother has guarded this simple garam masala recipe for years. I finally got her to divulge it for this book. I call it 'daal dust', as it magically tops any daal, and adds a haunting flavour. Store in an airtight jar for up to 3 months.

Grind together in a dry spice grinder
- 5cm/2-inch cinnamon stick
- 10–15 cloves
- 4–5 green cardamom pods

Chaat masala

A piquant blend that can transform the dullest dish to a heightened flavour experience: use it on eggs, lentils or even atop a cheese toastie. Store in an airtight jar for up to 3 months.

Grind together in a dry spice grinder
- 2 tbsp dry-roasted cumin seeds
- 1 tbsp kalanamak (black salt)
- 1½ tbsp amchoor (dried mango powder)
- 1–2 dried red chillies
- 1 tsp ground anardana (dried pomegranate)
- 1 tsp black peppercorns (optional)

Baluchi-style sajji masala

This can be used on lamb or chicken sajji (see p94). Store in an airtight container for up to 3 months.

Grind together in a dry spice grinder

- 2 tbsp cumin seeds
- 2 tbsp whole black peppercorns
- 6 green cardamom pods
- 3 tbsp coriander seeds
- ½ tsp each kalanamak (black salt), optional, and sea salt
- 1 tbsp amchoor (dried mango powder)
- 1 tbsp whole fennel seeds

Lahori-style chargha masala

This can be used on chicken chargha (see p101) or can be used on any other chicken roast (see p 94). Store in an airtight container for up to 3 months.

Grind together in a dry spice grinder

- 1 tsp black peppercorns
- 1 dried red chilli, crushed
- 1 tsp dry-roasted cumin seeds
- 1 tsp dry-roasted coriander seeds
- 1 tsp fennel seeds
- ½ tsp ajwain (carom seeds)
- 3–4 green cardamom pods
- 1 tsp amchoor (dried mango powder)
- 1 tsp ground anardana (dried pomegranate)

Dhania mirchi (coriander chilli paste masala)

This is my mother's recipe for a fragrant coriander seed and fresh chilli masala. It's simple and quick to make and is wonderful added to marinades, curries or vegetable stir-frys. Store in an airtight container in the fridge for up to 4 days.

Grind together in a wet spice grinder, adding 2 tbsp of water

- 1 tbsp dry-roasted coriander seeds
- 1 tbsp dry-roasted cumin
- 1–3 fresh red chillies
- ½ tsp ajwain (carom seeds)

Panch puran (five-spice blend)

A blend of five spices (seeds) inspired by Bangladeshi cooking. It's something my kitchen is never without. It's wonderful with vegetables – use it to infuse the cooking oil before adding ingredients.

Mix together

- 1 tbsp cumin seeds
- 1 tbsp kalonji seeds (nigella seeds)
- 1 tbsp green aniseed
- ½ tsp fenugreek seeds
- 1 tbsp brown mustard seeds

Awakening the senses
Breakfast

Waking up to hot, humid conditions and knowing you have to go out into the bustling, sweaty streets of a Pakistani city is enough of a reason to roll over and go back to sleep. Often it was purely the anticipation of a breakfast feast of sweet and savoury flavours that inspired me to rise and face the day.

When it comes to a traditional Pakistani breakfast (known as a 'halva puri'), you are spoilt for choice. There's light and fluffy khagina (scrambled eggs with tomatoes, coriander and green chillies), cholay ka salan (chickpea curry) and the tasty potato dish aloo ki bhujia – all mopped up with steaming, deep-fried puri breads (see p61). This breakfast scene is only complete with sweet cardamom-laced semolina halva and a hot cardamom chai to ease the heat.

I loved to go out with my cousins and friends to the old food streets of Lahore and Karachi to find the best breakfast and be tempted by the sweet, spicy and smoky scents of these dishes. On broken chairs with wobbly tables, we'd sit next to a massive vat and watch a cook masterfully flinging puris into the hot oil, waiting for them to puff up into balloons then dishing them out within seconds.

Pairing painfully sweet semolina halva with a mix of salty, smoky and spicy flavours may not sound like a natural mix, but the combination will surprise and delight the adventurous and sceptical alike. The oiliness of the puris with the heat of the curries and the sweetness of the halva kickstarts the taste buds, and the sugary carbohydrate boost awakens the senses.

Cholay ka salan

Chickpea curry with tomatoes

Preparation 15 minutes if using canned chickpeas | **Cooking** 30 minutes | **Serves** 4–6

4 tbsp sunflower oil

1 tsp cumin seeds

½ tsp aniseed

1 tsp coriander seeds

½ tsp mustard seeds

5–6 fresh curry leaves

1 red onion, finely chopped

1 tsp grated ginger

1 tsp crushed garlic

4 large tomatoes, deseeded and
    finely chopped

1 tbsp tomato purée

600g/1lb 5oz canned chickpeas,
    drained and rinsed (or use
    400g/14oz dried chickpeas,
    soaked overnight with ½ tsp
    bicarbonate of soda (baking soda)
    and rinsed before boiling for 30–40
    minutes over a low heat, until soft)

250ml/9 fl oz/1 cup water

1 tsp salt

2 tsp amchoor (dried mango powder)

2 tbsp chopped coriander (cilantro)
    leaves

1 green chilli, finely chopped

Heat the oil in a saucepan with a lid over a medium heat. When hot, add the cumin, aniseed, coriander seeds and mustard seeds and when they start to splutter, after about 30 seconds, add the curry leaves. Those will splutter immediately. Then add the onion, ginger and garlic and cook, stirring, for 5 minutes, or until the onion is light brown.

Add the tomatoes and tomato purée and cook, stirring, for 5–8 minutes, adding a splash of water if it becomes too dry. Once the tomatoes are soft and the oil rises to the top of the sauce add the chickpeas and measured water. Reduce the heat, cover the pan with the lid and cook for about 10 minutes. By now the water should have halved and the gravy should be thick. Add the salt, stir in the amchoor and top with the coriander and chopped chilli.

Kitchen secret

For a dry dish, omit the water and let the tomato base evaporate a little. But if you feel that the sauce is too watery, try mashing a few of the chickpeas and stirring through. These add thickness and texure.

Aloo ki bhujia

Spicy potatoes with nigella seeds and fenugreek

Preparation 10 minutes | **Cooking** 25–30 minutes | **Serves** 4–6

3 tbsp sunflower oil

1 red onion, finely chopped

1-cm/½-inch piece ginger, grated

2 garlic cloves, crushed

1 tsp cumin seeds

1 tsp kalonji (nigella seeds)

2 tbsp dried methi (fenugreek leaves)

3 medium tomatoes, roughly chopped

¾ tsp sea salt

½ tsp ground turmeric

¾ tsp red chilli powder

250g/9oz salad potatoes, peeled and
    cut into 1-cm/½-inch squares

250ml/9 fl oz/1 cup water

Heat the oil in a saucepan with a lid. When hot, add the onion, ginger and garlic and cook over a high heat for 5–7 minutes, or until the onion is golden.

Add the cumin, kalonji, dried methi leaves, tomatoes, salt, turmeric and chilli powder, then reduce the heat. Mix well and keep stirring as you cook for about 10 minutes, or until the oil rises to the surface and the tomatoes are soft.

Add the potatoes and water, stir and increase the heat to medium. Cover the pan with the lid and cook for 10–12 minutes, or until the potatoes are tender and the water has evaporated. Serve hot.

Khagina

Spicy scrambled eggs with tomatoes and coriander

Preparation 10 minutes | **Cooking** 5 minutes | **Serves** 6

6 medium eggs

6–7 cherry tomatoes, chopped

2 tbsp chopped coriander (cilantro) leaves

2 green chillies, finely chopped

1 spring onion (scallion), finely chopped

salt, to taste

2 tsp ghee or substitute with 1 tbsp butter and 1 tsp vegetable oil (see p23)

1½ tsp cumin seeds

2 garlic cloves, finely chopped

freshly ground pepper

1 tsp chaat masala (see p26)

Whisk the eggs in a bowl, then add the tomatoes, coriander, green chillies, spring onion and salt and stir to combine.

Heat the ghee or butter and oil in a frying pan over a medium heat. When hot, add the cumin seeds and fry for 30 seconds until they splutter.

Add the garlic and fry for a further 30–40 seconds until it is lightly browned. Add the egg mixture and scramble for 1–2 minutes until cooked. Serve immediately with freshly ground black pepper and chaat masala.

This dish, together with cholay ka salan and aloo ki bhujia (see p30) are best eaten with puri breads (see p61).

Sweet semolina halva

With pistachio and rose water

Preparation 15 minutes | **Cooking** 25 minutes | **Serves** 4–6

2 tbsp ghee (see p23)

2–3 green cardamom pods, seeds removed and ground

100g/3½ oz/½ cup coarse semolina

5 tbsp caster (superfine) sugar

150ml/5 fl oz/⅔ cup whole milk

1 tbsp chopped pistachios

1 tbsp raisins

3–4 drops rose water

rose petals and nuts, to decorate

Heat the ghee in a saucepan over a medium heat. When hot, add the ground cardamom and semolina and cook, stirring constantly for 5–6 minutes, or until the semolina is aromatic and infuses with the cardamom.

Stir in the sugar, then pour in the milk and add the nuts and raisins. Stir vigorously to prevent the mixture from sticking to the base of the pan. The semolina will puff up and come together and become very thick. Add a little more milk if it is too firm.

Stir the mixture for a further 3 minutes then turn off the heat and pour the semolina into a serving dish or individual moulds. Stir in the rose water and leave to set for a few minutes. Serve warm or at room temperature decorated with a sprinkling of rose petals and nuts.

Sabudana kheer

Tapioca pearls with coconut and pistachio dust

Sabudana kheer (tapioca pudding) is comfort in a bowl: as those milky pearls glide down my throat, I always feel I'm back home, safe and warm. It is a staple 'sehri' dish (this is the meal fasting Muslims eat before dawn), as it's satisfying and releases its energy slowly to help get you through the day. It can be served either warm or cold.

70g/2½ oz/½ cup tapioca pearls
500ml/17 fl oz/2 cups water
500ml/17 fl oz/2 cups whole milk
3 cardamom pods, seeds removed and finely ground
4–5 tbsp caster (superfine) sugar or light brown sugar
3 tbsp fine desiccated (dry unsweetened) coconut
2 tbsp finely ground pistachios (or any other nuts of choice)

Preparation 15 minutes + 15 minutes soaking | **Cooking** 25 minutes | **Serves** 4

Wash the tapioca pearls until the water runs clear, then soak in a bowl of water for 15 minutes. Drain and put the tapioca into a saucepan with the measured water and bring to the boil. Cook for 15 minutes, or until the tapioca pearls are soft, then remove from the heat and allow to cool. Meanwhile, heat the milk in a large heavy-based saucepan over a medium heat.

Once the tapioca is cooled, add it to the hot milk, then add the cardamom, sugar and half of the desiccated coconut and cook, stirring constantly for 5–6 minutes, or until the tapicoa begins to swell up and the mixture becomes thicker. Stir in half of the pistachios.

Pour the tapioca mixture into a large serving dish and decorate with the remaining ground pistachios and desiccated coconut.

Tantalising the taste buds
Street food and snacks

Walking through the streets of Pakistan is a complete sensory experience. The sights and smells tantalise the taste buds as nearly all activity on the pavement involves food, both raw and ready to eat.

Fruit and vegetable vendors shout out prices and are miraculously still heard above the deafening exhausts of rickshaws and the horns of buses and cars. And through bumper-to-bumper traffic, people find their way to a vendor's side, drawn in by aromatic smoke rising from their heavily laden stalls selling pakoras, samosas, haleem and biryanis. People in cars pull right up to open-air restaurants and seat themselves on fold-out furniture, while calling for chicken tikkas on the bone, kebab rolls and fresh naans from the tandoor.

Breathing in a cocktail of car fumes and barbecue smoke may sound unpleasant, but to me it's the essence of eating on the streets of Pakistan. This is a country where all food, be it a snack or a full meal, is available around the clock, served in your car at midnight or delivered to your home by a young waiter at 3am. Street food in Pakistan is a full-time love affair and it's this vibrant food culture which inspires the snacks in this chapter.

Some of them speak of childhood food stops on journeys to school, others are created from the love of piquant platefuls served hurriedly on kitsch plastic plates by streetside vendors or the dedicated 'thela-walas' – enterprising folk selling snacks on rickety stalls under the scorching sun.

Bhutta
Barbecued corn with chilli and lime

This simple street snack is tangled in my mind with memories of crisp winter evenings spent on the Karachi coast watching the sunset. Street food vendors serve these smoking-hot – and provide a lime to rub on the spices. If you're not barbecuing, just use a griddle pan indoors for a similar effect.

Preparation 15 minutes | **Cooking** 15–25 minutes | **Serves** 2–4

2 corn-on-the-cobs cut into 2 halves, cleaned
2 tsp butter or ghee, for brushing (see p23)
1 lime, quartered
1 tsp each of sea salt, red chilli powder and ground kalanamak (black salt) mixed together

Light a barbecue or preheat a griddle pan. Boil the corn in a saucepan of boiling water for 5–7 minutes, then remove with a slotted spoon and brush with the butter or ghee. Place the corn on the griddle or barbecue and keep turning and brushing with oil until all the sides are slightly blackened and the corn is cooked through, about 10 minutes.

To serve, dip the lime quarters into the chilli salt mixture and rub all over the hot corn.

Griddled dry chickpeas
With red chilli and salt masala

Over coals, street food vendors toss green husked chickpeas in hot sands taken up from the silver Seaview Beach in Karachi. Once chargrilled, they are served with a Himalayan kalanamak (black salt) spice blend that's detailed in the recipe above.

Preparation 5 minutes | **Cooking** 10 minutes | **Serves** 4–6

400g/14oz/1¾ cups chickpeas (if canned, drained; if dried, soaked overnight then drained)
3 tsp red chilli and salt masala from recipe above
½ lime

Heat a griddle pan until hot then reduce the heat to medium and add the drained chickpeas. Cook, stirring constantly, for 10 minutes until they start to brown, but don't stick to the griddle pan.

Once they appear chargrilled, serve them hot tossed in the red chilli and salt masala and a squeeze of lime juice.

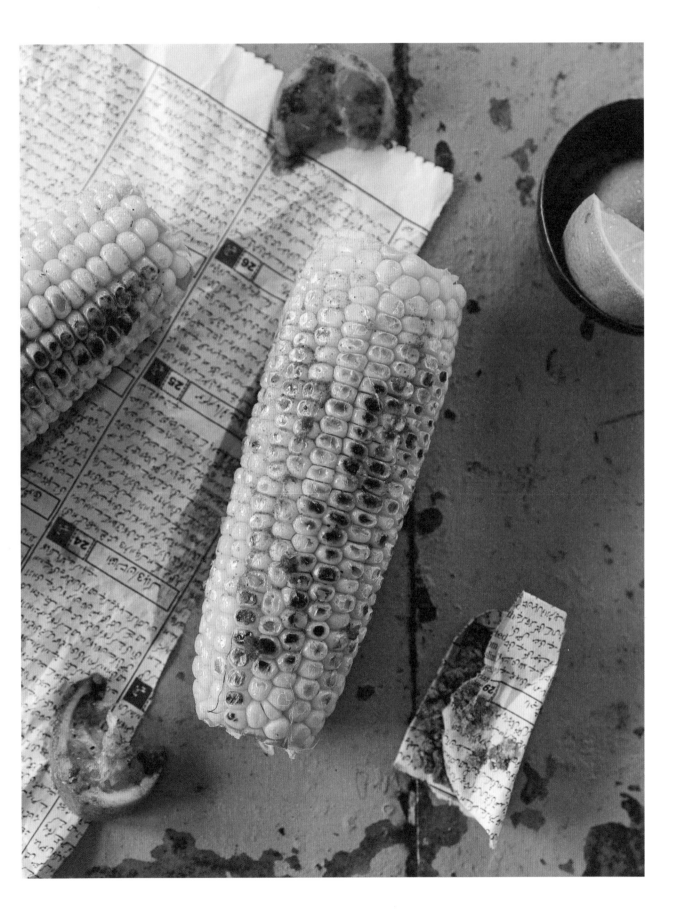

Hyderabadi-style samosas
Filled with red onion, mint and green chilli

I came across these samosas in the bustling Hyderabadi colony in Karachi – an area filled with immigrants from Hyderabad in India who settled there at the time of partition in 1947. Their cuisine is rich, aromatic and renowned in Pakistan as being very festive. The special ingredient here is pawa (a dried flattened rice), which soaks up all the juices from the onions, leaving tiny, crisp, moreish parcels of flavour.

For the filling

1–2 medium red onions, cut into
    fine half-moons
large handful of powa/poha (dried
    pressed rice, available in South
    Asian stores)
½ tsp chaat masala (see p26)
½ tsp red chilli powder
1 tsp dry-roasted cumin seeds
¾ tsp salt
handful of coriander (cilantro) leaves,
    roughly chopped
6–8 mint leaves, roughly chopped
1–2 thin green chillies, finely chopped
juice of ½ lemon

For the samosas

12 samosa sheets or filo pastry
    (phyllo dough) cut into 24 sheets
500ml/17 fl oz/2 cups sunflower oil,
    for frying, plus 2 tbsp sunflower
    oil, for sealing

Preparation 20 minutes | **Cooking** 15 minutes | **Makes about** 12 samosas

Add all the ingredients for the filling together in a bowl and toss to ensure they are mixed well. Set aside.

To assemble the samosas, lay out the samosa pastry (if using filo, use 2 sheets, stuck together with a light brush of oil). Samosa pastry is traditionally comes in narrow rectangles, making it easier to make a triangular samosa shape.

Brush the pastry facing you lightly with oil. Place 1 tablespoon of the filling on the top right-hand side of the pastry and begin to fold the remaining length of pastry up and over the filling to form a triangle shape. Keep folding up and across the remaining pastry until you have wrapped all the pastry.

Using the pastry brush, brush oil on the loose end of the pastry to seal the samosa. Repeat with the remaining pastry and filling to make about 12 samosas.

Heat the 500ml/17 fl oz/2 cups oil in a large, heavy-based deep pan over a medium heat to 180°C/350°F, or until a cube of bread sizzles in 30 seconds. Once the oil is smoking, reduce the heat to low. Carefully add the samosas to the hot oil in batches and deep-fry for 2–4 minutes until golden brown all over. Remove with a slotted spoon and drain on kitchen paper. Serve hot with a chutney or sauce, such as the green chutney on p146.

Spiced lentil bun kebabs

I'd crave these vegetarian kebabs-in-a-bun on hot afternoons – they define the explosive flavour of Pakistani street snacks, bringing together spiced tamarind and green chutney toppings. I had to drive to my favourite stall called Flamingo with my friend Shazia to buy the traditional version of this burger. It came hot in a greasy brown paper bag, begging to be devoured and then washed down with Pakola – a ubiquitous, green, saccharin-sweet fizzy soft drink.

For the burgers

60g/2oz/¼ cup chana daal

3 Maris Piper potatoes

3 egg whites, beaten to soft peaks

4 tbsp ghee (see p23)

6–8 tbsp vegetable oil

4–6 burger buns

6 tsp tamarind sauce (see p23)

6 tsp green chutney (see p146)

6 tbsp tomato ketchup or chilli
  garlic sauce

1–2 tomatoes, cut into round slices

½ cucumber, cut into thin
  round slices

For the spices

2 tsp ground cumin

1 tsp ground coriander (cilantro)

2 tsp chaat masala (see p26)

1 tsp red chilli powder

1 tsp sea salt, or to taste

Preparation 30 minutes + 30 minutes soaking | **Cooking** 50 minutes | **Serves** 4–6

Soak the chana daal in a bowl of water for 2 hours, then drain and boil in enough water to cover them for 30 minutes, or until soft. Drain and set aside. Meanwhile, peel the potatoes and boil in a large saucepan until soft.

To make the patties, mash the potatoes, spices, salt and cooked daal together in a large bowl using a fork. Using a tablespoon, scoop out 2 tablespoons of the spiced mash and form into 10cm/4-inch round burger-style patties.

Put the beaten egg white into a shallow bowl. Heat 1 tablespoon each of ghee and oil (this should be enough to cook 1 patty) in a non-stick frying pan over a medium-low heat. Dip each patty into the beaten egg white and fry for about 2–3 minutes on each side until light brown. Place each cooked patty on a plate and cover with another plate to keep warm.

Once all the patties are cooked and ready to serve, cut the burger buns in half. Heat about ½ teaspoon each of the ghee and vegetable oil in a flat griddle pan or frying pan and fry all 4 sides of each bun until caramelised and crispy, about 2 minutes on each side. Repeat until all the buns are fried.

To assemble the bun kebab, place a patty on the bottom fried bun, top with tamarind sauce (see p23), green chutney (see p146), tomato ketchup or chilli garlic sauce, and a slice of tomato and cucumber, if you like, then cover the burger with the top side of the bun. Serve with more of the sauces.

Apple pakoras spiced with chaat masala

As the sweltering days of summer melted into cooler evenings, I remember huddling under soft blankets with my Nani (maternal grandmother), breathing in Karachi's sea air and eating fresh pakoras. It's this memory that inspires my own tart yet comforting apple pakoras.

160g/5¾oz/1¾ cups gram flour
40g/1½oz/¼ cup rice flour
150ml/5 fl oz/⅔ cup water
1 tsp dry-roasted cumin seeds
1 tsp red chilli powder
1 tsp ground coriander
¾ tsp salt
1 tbsp chopped coriander (cilantro) leaves
1 tbsp chaat masala (see p26)
2 Granny Smith apples, peeled, cored and cut into thin round slices
500ml/17 fl oz/2 cups sunflower oil

Preparation 15 minutes | **Cooking** 10–15 minutes | **Serves** 5–6

Whisk the flours, water, all the spices, salt, coriander leaves and about 1 teaspoon of the chaat masala together in a large bowl until it is a thick batter. When the consistency is correct the batter should lazily fall off a spoon. Add the apple slices to the batter and mix well until the apple is coated evenly in the pakora batter.

Heat the oil for deep-frying in a deep, heavy-based pan over a medium heat to 180°C/350°F, or until a cube of bread sizzles in 30 seconds, then reduce the heat to low. Using your hands, pop 1 apple slice at a time into the oil and deep-fry on either side for 3–4 minutes. Drain on kitchen paper. Sprinkle with the remaining chaat masala to serve.

Shabbo Khala's cauliflower pakoras
With spiced moong daal batter

In Pakistan, a mother's closest friends are like maternal aunts and are called 'Khala'. Every Khala has her secret recipes – this one is my Shabbo Khala's. As a child I would excitedly anticipate meals at her house, hoping to get some of these thinly sliced cauliflower florets in spicy lentil batter.

150g/5oz/1½ cups moong daal
2 tbsp water
½ tsp red chilli powder
1 tsp salt
1 tsp cumin seeds
½ tsp ground turmeric
½ tsp ground coriander
½ tsp chaat masala (see p26)
1 tbsp chopped coriander (cilantro) leaves
150–200ml/5–7 fl oz/⅔–scant 1 cup vegetable oil
½ cauliflower, cut into florets then florets sliced thinly vertically

Preparation 25 minutes + 3–8 hours soaking | **Cooking** 10 minutes | **Serves** 6–8

To make the batter, soak the lentils in a bowl of water for at least 3 hours, or overnight, then drain and put them into a food processor or blender. Blend with the measured water until it is a smooth thick batter. Stir in all the spices, salt and chopped coriander.

Heat the oil in a wok-style pan over a medium heat. When the oil is smoking hot, reduce the heat to low.

Dip the slices of cauliflower into the batter (forming a thin coating of batter on the cauliflower) and deep-fry in the oil for 2 minutes, or until golden brown. Move the pakora around as they cook to allow them to cook evenly. Remove the pakoras with a slotted spoon and drain on kitchen paper. Serve immediately.

Mummy's dahi baras
Soft lentil dumplings topped with yogurt and tamarind

My earliest memories of Ramazan (the period of fasting for Muslims) are of my mother and I preparing iftar (a feast to break the fast at sunset). No iftar was complete without her dahi baras – cotton wool-soft lentil dumplings adorned with cool whipped buffalo yogurt. The nutty aroma of the lentil fritters being fried and then immediately plunged into water (which according to my mother ensures a softer fritter) takes me straight back to those days.

For the soft lentil fritters
220g/8oz/1 cup urid daal
2 tsp dry-roasted cumin seeds
1 tsp red chilli powder
salt, to taste
600ml/1 pint/2½ cups sunflower
    oil, for deep-frying

For the topping
500g/17oz/2 cups whole Greek
    yogurt
¾ tsp salt, or to taste
1 tsp caster (superfine) sugar
¼ tsp grated or crushed garlic
1 small red onion, cut into
    rings (Tip: soak in water
    for 10 minutes before use
    to remove the strong onion
    aroma)
2–3 tbsp tamarind sauce (see p23)
1 tsp chaat masala (see p26)
½ tsp red chilli powder
1 tsp dry-roasted cumin seeds
handful of coriander (cilantro)
    leaves, chopped
1 green chilli, chopped
1-cm/½-inch piece ginger, peeled
    and cut into julienne
7–8 mint sprigs, chopped

Preparation 30 minutes + overnight soaking | **Cooking** 25 minutes | **Serves** 7–8

Soak the lentils overnight in a bowl of water in a warm place. The next day, make sure that the soaked lentils have a fermented smell and the water appears bubbly. Drain and reserve the water. Put the lentils into a bowl and add the cumin, chilli powder and salt and blend into a fine paste, which should resemble thick hummus. If it is very thick, then add 1 teaspoon of the reserved water. Set aside for 10 minutes.

Heat the oil for deep-frying the fritters in a wok-style pan over a medium heat to 180°C/350°F, or until a cube of bread sizzles in 30 seconds, then reduce the heat to very low. The idea is not to have the oil hot enough so as to cook the outside of the fritter and not the inside. Keep a bowl of cool water nearby.

Put 1 teaspoon of the batter into the hot oil (that is enough, as they double in size as they cook and you are looking to create a flattish, round fritter). Fry in batches, 3–4 at a time, so there is still a free movement of fritters. While cooking, if you make a small hole in the fritter with a knife, they cook faster. Continue to fry gently until medium brown on the outside and cooked through. Once they are cooked, drop them into the bowl of water immediately and leave for 2 minutes, then remove and squeeze the excess water out. Arrange in a serving dish.

To assemble the dish, whisk the yogurt together with the salt, sugar and garlic. Pour this over the soft fritters in the serving dish. Garnish with the red onion, tamarind sauce (see p23), chaat masala (see p26), red chilli powder, cumin, chopped coriander, chilli, ginger and mint. Serve cool.

Kitchen secret
These fritters freeze well. After squeezing out the water, place them in an airtight container and freeze for up to 3 months. Ensure they are defrosted completely before adding the spiced toppings.

Kat-a-kat

Stir-fried and steamed chicken livers and kidneys

The streets of Karachi come alive at night with the aroma of barbecues and sounds of chatter, cars and cooking. One particular combination of smell and sound is 'kat-a-kat'. The dish is made on a large flat pan over a huge gas fire, and its ingredients are added alongside splashes of water and butter so that plumes of steam rise and its fragrance fills the air. The meat is then cut using two metal knives and bashed about on the pan creating the iconic 'kat-a-kat' sound.

For the kat-a-kat garam masala

1 tsp cumin seeds
½ tsp green aniseed
1 tsp dried methi (fenugreek) leaves
¼ tsp ground mace
1½ tsp red chilli powder
1 tbsp coriander (cilantro) seeds
¼ tsp ground turmeric

For the kat-a-kat

4cm/1½-inch cinnamon stick
5 chicken livers
5 chicken kidneys
1 skinless, boneless chicken breast
    (or 6 chicken wings)
¾ tsp salt, or to taste
2 tsp grated ginger
½ tsp crushed garlic
2 tbsp ghee or unsalted butter
    (see p23)
2 onions, roughly chopped
3 small tomatoes, roughly chopped
a bunch of coriander (cilantro),
    chopped
2.5cm/1-inch piece ginger, peeled
    and cut into julienne
4 green chillies, chopped
juice of ½ lemon

Preparation 15–25 minutes | **Cooking** 20 minutes | **Serves** 2–4

Grind all the spices for the kat-a-kat garam masala in a spice grinder until ground. Set aside.

Wash the livers, kidneys and chicken breast well before cutting into small bite-sized pieces. Dry on kitchen paper.

In a bowl, combine the livers, kidneys, chicken breast, the ground kat-a-kat masala, salt, ginger paste and garlic paste. Heat a wok over a medium heat but do not add any ghee or butter. Add the meat mixture and a splash of water and stir-fry for 10 minutes.

Heat the ghee or butter in another frying pan or wok over a medium heat. When hot, add the onions and fry until they are translucent. Add the tomatoes and meats and fry for a further 5–10 minutes until the meats are tender. Serve garnished with coriander leaves, ginger and green chillies, lemon juice and any remaining masala sprinkled on top.

Kitchen secret

This dish is traditionally made with lamb's liver, heart, brain and kidneys, but you can make it with a combination of chicken breast and chicken wings alone.

Beef kebab rolls
With chutney and salad

While the word 'kebab' conjures up images of terrible takeaways, the history of the dish is a romantic marriage of Persian and Arabic food traditions. Pakistan's obsession with grilled meat has meant these kebab rolls (a simple dish of parathas, beef and chutney) can be found at many food stalls.

For the kebabs

250g/9oz beef mince (ground beef)
1 red onion, finely chopped
2.5-cm/1-inch piece ginger, peeled and grated
2 green chillies, finely chopped
2 tbsp chopped coriander (cilantro) leaves
1 tsp garam masala (see p26)
salt, to taste
2 tbsp sunflower oil, for frying

For the parathas

225g/8oz/1⅔ cups wholewheat flour
a pinch of salt
150ml/5 fl oz/⅔ cup warm water (or as much water as required to make a soft dough)
2 tbsp ghee (see p23)

For the topping

1 tbsp green chutney (see p146)
1 tbsp tamarind sauce (see p23)
½ red onion, thinly sliced
1 large tomato, chopped

Preparation 30 minutes + 30 minutes standing | **Cooking** 15–20 minutes | **Serves** 8

Combine all the ingredients for the kebabs together, except the oil. Place in a food processor and process for 1 minute. To form the kebabs, divide the mince into 8 equal portions, about 3 tablespoons of mince for each kebab. Roll each portion into the shape of a sausage, about 7.5cm/3 inches long and 1cm/½ inch wide.

To cook the kebabs, heat the oil in a large frying pan with a lid over a high heat, then reduce the heat to medium low and shallow-fry in batches, partially covered for about 10 minutes, or until all the moisture dries up and the kebabs are cooked through. Turn the kebabs frequently until all the sides are browned and cooked.

Sift the wholewheat flour and salt together. Add the water and knead it into a soft dough then set aside for about 30 minutes.

Divide the dough into 8 equal parts. Placing one portion of dough in your palm, roll into a ball. If your hands get sticky, rub a little ghee on to your hands. Continue to do this until you have 8 smooth balls. Cover with a damp tea towel or clingfilm.

To make the parathas, lightly dust a clean surface with flour, and roll out one dough ball into a circle, about 10cm/4 inches wide. Smear about ½ teaspoon ghee in the middle of the dough and roll up into a long sausage. Next, wind up the sausage to make a spiral, like a cinnamon roll shape. Flatten the spiral with your palm, dip in a little flour, then roll out no larger than 13cm/5 inches. Heat a tava, flat griddle pan or pancake pan over a high heat. When hot, reduce the heat to medium and smear on ½ teaspoon ghee. Place the paratha on to the pan and, using kitchen paper, press down to ensure even cooking. When tiny bubbles are rising on the top, about 2 minutes, turn the paratha over and pour a little ghee around the sides. Press down the paratha evenly with kitchen paper. When both sides are light brown, it is ready. This will take about 3–5 minutes. Repeat until all the parathas are cooked. Place them in foil to keep warm if not eating straight away.

To serve, put 1–2 kebabs in the middle of the paratha, then pour over chutney (see p146), ketchup and tamarind sauce (see p23). Place on onion slices and tomato then roll up.

Shakarkandi
Baked sweet potato with chaat masala

An eagerly awaited winter snack, these coal-baked sweet potatoes are served with nothing more than a sprinkle of chaat masala and a squeeze of lemon. They're hawked from wooden carts with a steel tub that's used to barbecue the potatoes, and they're handed out wrapped in paper.

2 large sweet potatoes
2 tsp chaat masala (see p26)
½ lemon

Preparation 10 minutes | **Cooking** 60–70 minutes | **Serves** 2–4

Preheat the oven to 200°C/400°F/gas mark 6.

Pierce the sweet potatoes with a fork then wrap each one in a piece of foil. Place them on the middle shelf of the oven and bake for 60–75 minutes, or until tender.

To serve, cut the sweet potatoes in half or into chunks and sprinkle with chaat masala and a squeeze of lemon juice, if you like.

Himalayan spiced fried eggs

This dish may not sound elaborate, but the fried eggs topped with a Himalayan black salt-based chaat masala is an incredible combination. This sulphuric tangy blend brings the humble egg to life.

5 tbsp sunflower oil
2 eggs
1 tsp chaat masala (see p26)

Preparation 5 minutes | **Cooking** 5 minutes | **Serves** 1

Heat the oil in a frying pan over a medium heat and fry the eggs as liked. Top with a sprinkling of chaat masala and serve.

Breaking bread and sharing rice

Breads and rice dishes

The busy day comes to a deadening halt, shutters are pulled down on shops, and office workers break free from their stations. All is put on hold as people sit together to enjoy this simple pleasure: the sharing of food. No one in Pakistan would question the momentous nature of this daily occurrence. Work can wait, lunch comes first.

In fact, if there is one unifying feature that crosses all boundaries of the disparate Pakistani people, it would be the love of breaking bread and sharing rice. There's an understanding that all men are equal when it comes to this experience, whether it be mopping up a daal with chapati, dipping naan in a bowl of haleem or tucking into a biryani lunch.

Bread and rice is the lifeblood of the Pakistani people: it is these staples that fills everyone's table, from wealthy businessmen to the farmers tending fields ablaze with golden wheat on fertile Punjabi plains, and the labourer working on vulnerable paddy fields of basmati, where livelihood relies on the monsoon downpours.

The recipes in this chapter are ones I grew up cooking at home. Some were taught to me with precision, while others I learned by watching and eating. But it's theses dishes that form the central part of any meal I make, be it a simple weekday dinner or a feast for special guests.

When you come to make the rice dishes, it's worth investing in good rice. With basmati, the quality and age of the rice (as well as pre-soaking it) have a big impact on how long the dish takes to cook, especially when cooking by absorption. The times given in these recipes are based on using pre-soaked, premium-quality, long-grain basmati rice which is between one and two years old. This cooks fast and produces fluffy, unbroken grains. If you're using basic-quality, younger rice, you'll need to adjust the cooking times: add a further 2–3 minutes to par-boiling times, and add a further 5–6 minutes to the final pulao cooking time.

Sweet potato and squash parathas

These aren't your typical stuffed parathas: instead they're more like Scottish tattie scones in which mashed potato is mixed with flour to make flat griddle scones, although these are much thinner. This recipe is quicker and easier than making stuffed parathas, but has the same comforting result.

50g/1¾ oz mashed sweet potato

25g/1oz steamed and mashed butternut squash

100g/3½ oz/¾ cup plain (all-purpose) flour, plus extra for dusting

½ tsp salt

½ tsp ground turmeric

1 tsp dry-roasted cumin seeds

2 tbsp finely chopped coriander (cilantro) leaves

6 mint leaves, finely chopped

1 green chilli, finely chopped or ½ tsp red chilli flakes

2 spring onions (scallions), finely chopped

1 tbsp amchoor (dried mango powder) or juice of ½ lime

3–4 tbsp ghee (see p23)

Preparation 30 minutes | **Cooking** 10 minutes | **Makes** 6

Mix all the ingredients together, except the ghee, in a large bowl. Slowly add the ghee a little at a time, mixing, until all the ingredients begin to come together to form a firm dough-like consistency. You will need to knead it for a few minutes until all the ingredients come together, then turn out on to a floured work surface and knead the dough until smooth.

Divide the dough into a tennis ball-sized portions and shape into round balls. Keep the balls covered with a damp cloth.

Heat a flat griddle pan, tawa or frying pan over a high heat. When hot, add a little ghee then reduce the heat to medium.

Roll out each ball into a 5 mm/¼ inch flat round paratha on a floured surface. Carefully place in the hot ghee and cook gently pressing down the corners of the paratha with a clean tea towel or kitchen paper, to ensure that the paratha browns evenly.

When one side is cooked, about 3–4 minutes, turn over and cook the other side. Repeat until all the parathas are made. Serve immediately with yogurt, raita or pickle. They are also lovely with some hot tea!

Kitchen secret

When making any flatbread, using a large piece of foil to cover the cooked breads will keep them soft and warm. Put it over a plate or roll up the breads into the piece of foil completely until ready to eat.

Tandoori roti

A tandoori roti is the most common bread in Pakistan and is a flatbread much like a chapati, but it's cooked in the 'tandoor' (a clay oven) rather than in a pan on the hob. It's thicker and more filling than a chapati, but lighter than naan. Make these under a hot grill for the best results.

Preparation 10 minutes + 30 minutes resting | **Cooking** 15 minutes | **Makes** 6

500g/1lb 2oz/4¼ cups chapati flour or wholewheat flour, plus extra for dusting
½ tsp salt
240ml/8 fl oz/1 cup water
1 tbsp ghee or oil (see p23)

Mix the flour and salt together in a bowl until combined. Pour in the measured water to make a soft dough. Allow to rest for about 30 minutes.

Preheat the grill. Heat a flat non-stick tawa pan, pancake pan or frying pan with an ovenproof handle over a high heat. When hot reduce the heat to medium. Divide the dough into tennis ball-sized portions and roll them into balls. On a floured surface, using a rolling pin, roll a ball into a thin flatbread about 3–4 mm/⅛ inch thick. Then cook each for about 2–3 minutes until the bottom of the bread is light brown. Put the pan with the bread under the grill for 3–5 minutes until the top is light brown and cooked. Keep covered in a foil pouch until all the roti are ready. Serve hot.

Naan with nigella and sesame seeds

Preparation 20 minutes + 1–3 hours resting | **Cooking** 15 minutes | **Makes** 6

320g/11oz/2¼ cups organic strong plain flour, plus extra for dusting
a pinch of salt
1 tsp baking powder
¼ tsp bicarbonate of soda (baking soda)
1 tsp caster (superfine) sugar
1 egg, beaten
2 tbsp ghee, plus extra for coating (see p23)
100ml/3½ fl oz/scant ½ cup beaten plain yogurt
about 300ml/10 fl oz/1¼ cups whole milk

For the spice toppings
½ tsp each of nigella seeds and sesame seeds or 1 tsp each of chopped coriander (cilantro) leaves, mint, dill and chopped green chillies

Sift the flour, salt, baking powder, bicarbonate of soda and sugar together in a large bowl. Make a well in the middle and pour in the beaten egg and 1 tablespoon ghee and work the dough into a ball. Add the yogurt and half the milk and knead to make a smooth dough. You may need to add a little more milk. If using a stand mixer, put all the ingredients into the bowl and knead with a dough hook until a dough is formed. Knead the dough very well until smooth then coat it lightly with a little ghee. Allow to rest in a warm place, covered with a damp tea towel, for at least 1 hour, or up to 3 hours. The dough should have risen, but not quite doubled in size.

Knead the dough again briefly then divide into 7–8 small, round balls. Using a rolling pin, roll the dough into an oblong naan with a tapering end then pierce with a fork all over. Brush the naans lightly with ghee and sprinkle with your choice of seeds, spices or fresh herbs. Preheat a grill to high. Heat a dry heavy-based non-stick frying pan over a high heat and slap on the naan. Cook for 1–2 minutes until the naan is lightly browned underneath then cook under the hot grill for 5–7 minutes until it puffs up and is light brown on the top. Repeat until all the naans are cooked, then serve.

Makkai ki roti with makhan

Corn flatbread with homemade butter

Traditionally eaten in the Punjab province, this unleavened corn bread is a staple in rural villages. It can be topped with mustard pickle, or freshly made makhan butter (made from buffalo milk or cream).

400g/14oz/3½ cups cornmeal or fine polenta

1 pinch salt

½ tsp caster (superfine) sugar

about 50ml/2 fl oz/ scant ¼ cup water

2 tbsp ghee (see p23)

1½ tbsp homemade makhan butter (see recipe below)

For the makhan

100ml/3½ fl oz/scant ½ cup buffalo milk if available (or double/heavy cream)

Preparation 15 minutes + 10 minutes resting | **Cooking** 15 minutes | **Makes** 6

Mix the cornmeal, salt and sugar together in a large bowl with a fork. Add enough water to make a soft dough. Knead lightly then cover and allow to rest for 10 minutes.

To make the makhan, put the milk or cream into a plastic container with a lid, seal with the lid and shake vigorously until it comes together to form a thick butter-like consistency: about 6–8 minutes of shaking. You can also use an electric whisk and whisk for about 3–5 minutes until it turns into butter.

To cook the flatbreads, heat a flat frying pan or pancake pan over a medium heat. Add about 1 teaspoon of ghee and let it melt, then reduce the heat to low.

Dust a little cornmeal over a work surface. Divide the dough into golf-ball-sized balls, then using a rolling pin, roll each ball into a flatbread about 13–15cm/5–6 inches in diameter. Put one carefully into the hot pan and cook for about 3–4 minutes on each side until lightly brown in places. Remove and keep warm while the other dough balls are rolled out and cooked. Serve with a small piece of the makhan and with sarson ka saag on p134.

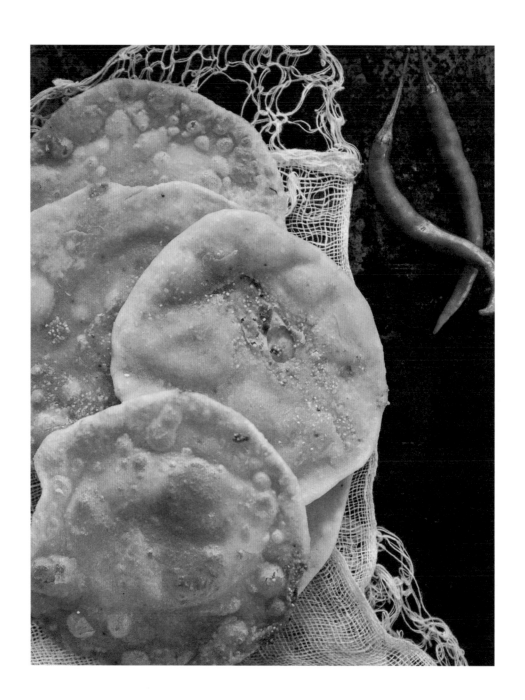

Dadi's puris

With poppy seeds and green chilli

This is my Dadi's (paternal grandmother) recipe – it has a delicate poppy seed, green chilli and ginger paste stuffed into a puri flatbread. It's best eaten with chutney, and is perfect at any time of day.

2 tbsp white poppy seeds

2 tbsp black poppy seeds

2–3 green chillies

2.5-cm/1-inch piece ginger, peeled

1 tbsp cumin seeds, dry-roasted before grinding

500g/1lb 2oz/4¼ cups unbleached wholemeal flour (atta) – you can buy this in Indian shops

salt, to taste

about 50–60ml/2–2¼ fl oz/ scant ¼– ¼ cup water

2 tbsp ghee (see p23)

50ml/2 fl oz/scant ¼ cup vegetable oil, for frying

Preparation 25 minutes + 24½ hours soaking & resting | **Cooking** 20 minutes | **Makes** 5–8

Soak the poppy seeds in a bowl of water for 24 hours, then drain and put into a small wet grinder or food processor. Add the green chilli, ginger and dry-roasted cumin seeds and grind until smooth.

Mix the wholemeal flour and a pinch of salt together in a large bowl. Make a well in the middle and pour in enough water to make a dough. Knead for 3–4 minutes until it forms a soft to firm dough. Add 1 teaspoon ghee, then cover with clingfilm and allow to rest for about 15–30 minutes.

Divide the dough into golf ball-sized portions then roll out with a rolling pin to make a small, thick round. Add the poppy seed mixture, bring the sides together and carefully close it up making sure that the mixture can not escape. Roll out again into small, thin 10×10cm/4×4-inch rounds.

Heat the oil in a large wok-style pan over a high heat to 180°C/350°F, or until a cube of bread sizzles in 30 seconds, then reduce the heat to medium-low (do this before you roll out the puris, so that the oil is sufficiently hot, then turn down the heat to maintain temperature).

Pop the puris, one by one, into the hot oil, pressing the puri down with a ladle into the oil, then quickly turn over and allow to cook well for 2–3 minutes. A sign to know when it's done is when the puri floats to the top and are very pale brown and crispy. Remove the puris with a slotted spoon and drain on kitchen paper. Serve immediately.

Whole garam masala and mutton pulao

This mutton pulao is what's traditionally known as 'yakhni' pulao (yakhni is a spiced meat or poultry-based stock), and in these pulaos the rice is cooked in a stock using the absorption method (as opposed to cooking rice in water and draining it). This dish can be both a festive and everyday dish, and is an ideal one-pot meal that can be served with a raita or salad.

250g/9oz/1¼ cups basmati rice
100ml/4 fl oz/½ scant cup
  sunflower or corn oil, used in
  two stages
1 tsp black peppercorns
1 medium cinnamon stick
1 tsp aniseed or star anise
1 tsp cloves
1 large black cardamon pod (optional)
3–4 green cardamom pods
400g/14oz mutton pieces with bone
2 tsp cumin seeds
1 tsp coriander (cilantro) seeds
2 bay leaves
2 large red onions, thinly sliced
1 tsp each of grated ginger and
  crushed garlic
salt, to taste
1 green chilli, chopped (optional)

Preparation 20 minutes + 30 minutes soaking | **Cooking** 60-70 minutes | **Serves** 4–6

Wash the rice, rinse and soak in a bowl of water for 30 minutes, then drain.

Heat half of the oil in a large saucepan with a lid over a medium heat. When hot, add the peppercorns, cinnamon, star anise, cloves and cardamom, and fry for 30 seconds, or until fragrant. Add the mutton and seal for 1–2 minutes, then add 500–600ml/1 pint/2–2½ cups water. Bring to a boil, lower the heat, cover the pan and cook until meat is tender, around 40-50 minutes.

As the mutton cooks, keep the water in the saucepan topped up, as you'll need the liquid later to use as a stock. When the mutton is cooked, drain the meat (being careful to reserve the stock) and discard the whole spices. You should have roughly 350ml/12 fl oz/1½ cups reserved stock. Set the meat and stock aside.

Using the same (now empty) saucepan, heat the remaining oil. When hot, add the cumin, coriander and bay leaves and fry for 30 seconds. Then add the onions, ginger and garlic, and stir-fry over a medium-low heat for 5–6 minutes until the onions are caramelised and brown.

Next, add the cooked mutton pieces and the drained rice to the onion mix. Add salt to taste. Stir gently for 1 minute. Then pour 300ml/10 fl oz/1¼ cups of the reserved stock over the meat and rice (you can freeze the rest for use in other dishes). This should just cover both. Reduce the heat to low. Cover the pan with a tight-fitting lid and allow to cook for about 8–10 minutes, or until the rice is cooked. The liquid should be completely absorbed. If the rice isn't cooked, add a splash (or 1 tablespoon) of water, cover the pan and cook for a further 1-2 minutes.

When cooked, fluff up the rice with a fork, stir through gently, garnish with the chopped green chilli and serve hot with a raita.

Kitchri

Lentil and basmati rice

This is comfort in a pot. Traditionally made for a loved one who is unwell, it helps soothe poorly tummies. It's simple flavours aren't just for the sick though – it's a dish that's said to have inspired the recipe for kedgeree, which was developed during the reign of the British Raj. I enjoy it with yogurt karri (p141) or plain yogurt.

150g/5oz/1½ cups moong daal (husked)
250g/9oz/1¼ cups basmati rice
salt, to taste
1 tbsp butter mixed with a teaspoon of oil or 1 tbsp ghee (see p23)
1 tsp cumin seeds
1 garlic clove, thinly sliced
1 small red onion, cut into rings

Preparation 10–12 minutes + 20 minutes soaking | **Cooking** 15–20 minutes | **Serves** 4–6

Mix the daal and rice together in a large sieve and rinse well, then put them into a bowl and pour in enough water to cover. Soak together for at least 20 minutes (you can leave it up to 1 hour, as the longer they are left soaking, the quicker they will cook).

Drain the rice and daal, put into a large saucepan and pour in 200–250ml/7–9 fl oz/ scant–1 cup water, or enough to cover the rice. Add salt, and bring to the boil then reduce the heat and simmer until the daal and rice are cooked and all the water has evaporated, about 10 minutes. The rice shouldn't be mushy and the daal should still have a bite. Take off the heat and set aside.

Heat the butter and oil or ghee in a small frying pan over a medium heat. When hot, add the cumin and fry for 30 seconds until it splutters. Add the garlic and fry until it is slightly crispy. Add the onion and fry for a further 2–3 minutes, or until the onion is soft.

Pour the flavoured butter/ghee mixture over the rice and daal and stir well. Serve with some plain Greek yogurt or whole plain yogurt, or if you can find it, thick buffalo milk yogurt.

Attock chana rijai

Chickpea and cumin pulao with brown rice

A wonderfully warm dish, this pulao has a recipe which was passed on to me by my friend Moneeza, whose father is from Attock. This pulao is cooked in a stock made with caramelised onions and spices. The addition of chickpeas and the use of brown basmati rice makes it a healthy dish – and well known for soothing a sore tummy (just leave out the green chilli). I've adapted this recipe by adding black cardamom and star anise: it makes it even more earthy and smoky.

250g/9oz/1¼ cups brown basmati rice
2 tbsp ghee (see p23)
2 tsp cumin seeds
1 star anise
1 tsp whole black peppercorns
1 black cardamom pod
2 large red onions, cut into half moons
1 tsp each of crushed garlic and grated ginger
2 x 400g/14oz cans chickpeas or 300g/10½ oz/1⅔ cups dried chickpeas, soaked overnight and boiled
salt, to taste
2 green chillies, deseeded and finely chopped
25 ml/1 fl oz/2 tbsp water

Preparation 15 minutes + 1 hour soaking | **Cooking** 40 minutes | **Serves** 4–6

Wash the rice, rinse and soak in a bowl of water for 1 hour, then drain.

Heat the ghee in a saucepan with a lid over a medium heat until melted. Add the cumin, star anise, peppercorns and black cardamom and fry for about 30 seconds until the ghee is fragrant, or until the cumin begins to pop.

Add the onions, garlic and ginger and fry, stirring over a medium heat for 3–4 minutes until the onions are soft and light brown. Add the drained chickpeas, salt and green chilli and fry for a further 30 seconds.

Add the drained rice, stir and mix for about 1 minute, then pour in 250ml/9 fl oz/1 cup water, or enough water to cover the rice. Reduce the heat to low, cover the saucepan with the lid and cook for about 4–5 minutes in order to par-cook the rice.

Once par-cooked the water should be almost absorbed. If it's totally absorbed add 25ml/1 fl oz/2 tbsp water, stir gently. Cover the pan with foil firmly around the edges, cover tightly with the lid, reduce the heat to as low, and let it cook in its own steam for about 10–12 minutes until the rice is cooked through and all the water has been absorbed. Serve with Greek yogurt.

Afghani lamb pulao

With sweet-sour raisins and carrots

Pakistan is home to many Afghan immigrants, and their cuisine is popular. This flavour-rich rice is made with meat stock and fragrant ground cardamom – and sweet-sour carrots and raisins lace each bite. Every Afghan family has their own recipe for Kabuli pulao, as it's also known, and this one is a mixture of a few I've adapted from different Afghan friends.

150ml/5 fl oz/⅔ cup vegetable oil
1 large red onion, finely chopped
4 tsp grated ginger
3 tsp crushed garlic
1 tbsp salt, more to taste
400g/14oz lamb leg or shoulder, on the bone, cut into 7.5-cm/3-inch pieces
1 litre/1¾ pints/4 cups water
300g/10½ oz/1⅔ cups basmati rice
70g/2½ oz/⅓ cup caster (superfine) sugar
2 tsp garam masala (make fresh by grinding together 1 tsp each of cloves, green cardamom pods, 4 bay leaves and 1cm/½-inch cinnamon stick)
1 tsp freshly ground cardamom
20g/¾oz carrots, peeled and cut into thin batons (sticks)
70g/2½oz/scant ½ cup sultanas (golden raisins) or raisins
handful of blanched almonds

Preparation 30–40 minutes + 1 hour soaking | **Cooking** 1 hour 15 minutes | **Serves** 6–8

To make the lamb stock, heat half the oil in a large saucepan over a medium heat. Add the onion and cook for 5–7 minutes until golden brown. Add the ginger, garlic and 1 tablespoon of salt and cook for 30 seconds until the raw garlic smell disappears.

Add the lamb and cook for 10 minutes, or until the meat is sealed and light brown. Pour in the measured water, then reduce the heat to low and cook gently for 1 hour, skimming the surface occasionally to remove any scum, until the lamb is tender. Remove the lamb from the pan and set aside. Reserve the stock. Meanwhile wash the rice, rinse and soak in a bowl of water for 1 hour. Then par-boil in hot salted water for 3–4 minutes.

Heat another saucepan over a medium heat and add half of the sugar. Cook, shaking the pan, for 5–6 minutes, or until the sugar has caramelised. Add 250ml/9 fl oz/1 cup of the reserved stock (freeze any leftover stock for another recipe), 1 teaspoon garam masala and ½ teaspoon ground cardamom. Bring to the boil, then remove from the heat.

Drain the par-boiled rice and put into the empty stock pan. Pour over the caramelised sugar mixture, add a 1 teaspoon garam masala and a pinch of cardamom, and stir until the rice is evenly coated. Remove from the heat.

To make the caramelised carrots, heat 1 tablespoon of the oil in a frying pan over a medium-high heat. Add the carrots and remaining sugar and stir-fry for 5 minutes, or until lightly caramelised. Add the sultanas and cook for 1 minute. Remove from the heat and stir in another pinch of cardamom. Set aside.

Heat the remaining oil in a frying pan until smoking hot. Pour the oil over the rice (enough to cover the rice evenly but not soak it). Make holes all over the rice with the back of a spoon to allow the rice to steam evenly, then scatter most of the carrot over the top. Place the lamb around the rice. Cover the pan firmly with foil and then with the lid. Place over a medium heat and cook for 8–10 minutes. The rice should be fluffy and fragrant, if still undercooked, cover and cook for a further 2 minutes. To serve, carefully spoon the rice and lamb on to a serving platter and garnish with almonds and remaining carrots and sultanas.

Mummy's nutty saffron rice

I was never fond of raisins and rice as a child, but as my taste buds matured I realised that my mother's Persian-influenced recipe is a spectacular yet simple midweek rice dish – a good accompaniment to something like the Kashmiri-style leg of lamb on p174. The saffron is infused in the water that cooks the rice, much like a pulao, and it gives the final dish a rather elegant biryani look.

½ tsp saffron threads
250g/9oz/1¼ cups basmati rice
5 tbsp vegetable oil
½ cinnamon stick
4–5 green cardamom pods, bashed open
6–7 cloves
I bay leaf
½ tsp black peppercorns
½ tsp salt, or to taste

For the nut and sultana mix
½ tbsp ghee, for frying (see p23)
handful each of shelled unsalted pistachios, skinned whole almonds and sultanas (golden raisins)
4 tbsp vegetable oil
I red onion, cut into thin rings

Preparation 20 minutes + 30 minutes soaking | **Cooking** 35–40 minutes | **Serves** 4–6

Soak the saffron in a bowl of hot water for 30 minutes. Wash the rice, rinse and soak in another bowl of cold water for at least 30 minutes, then drain.

To make the garnish for the rice, start by heating the ghee in a small frying pan over a medium heat. Add the nuts and allow to brown lightly, then add the sultanas and heat through until puffy. Set aside.

Then heat the oil in a shallow frying pan over a medium heat. When hot, add the onions and fry for 7–8 minutes until medium brown. Remove and drain on kitchen paper then set aside.

For the rice, heat about 2 tablespoons vegetable oil in a saucepan with a lid over a medium heat. When hot, add all the whole spices and fry for 30 seconds, or until they start to splutter. Add 800ml/28 fl oz/3½ cup water to the oil and spices, bring to a boil. Add the saffron and drained rice. Make sure the rice is well covered by the water, add more if necessary. The water should turn a light yellow.

Reduce the heat to medium-low. After about 4-5 minutes check to see if the rice is cooked. If not, replace the lid and cook for a further 2–3 minutes until done. Drain the rice and leave in the sieve for 2–3 minutes until all the moisture has evaporated and the rice is light and fluffy.

Transfer to a platter and serve, garnished with the nuts, raisins and browned onions.

Beef meatball pulao
With silver leaf and rose buds

This simple recipe for spiced pulao is made into something extra special with the addition of beef meatballs that are adorned with silver leaf for an eye-catching effect. The idea is that they're supposed to resemble pearls, and the recipe is known as 'motti' (pearl) pulao in my home. The silver-leaf can be left off, of course.

For the meatballs
300g/10½ oz beef mince
   (ground beef)
½ tsp each of grated ginger and garlic
1 tsp salt
1 tsp dry-roasted cumin seeds
½ tsp red chilli powder
1 tbsp breadcrumbs
vegetable oil, for frying

For the rice
250g/9oz/1¼ cups basmati rice
2 tbsp ghee (see p23)
2 tsp cumin seeds
1 star anise
1 tsp whole black peppercorns
1 black cardamom pod
2 large red onions, cut into
   half moons
1 tsp each of crushed garlic and
   grated ginger
2 green chillies, deseeded and
   finely chopped
salt, to taste
25ml/1 fl oz/2 tbsp water (optional)

To garnish
1 sheet edible silver leaf
10–12 dried edible rose buds

Preparation 25 minutes + 1 hour soaking | **Cooking** 40–45 minutes | **Serves** 4–6

Wash the rice, rinse and soak in a bowl of water for 1 hour, then drain.

Mix all the ingredients for the meatballs together in a bowl then divide the mixture into golf ball-sized balls. Heat the oil in a frying pan over a medium heat and cook the meatballs in batches for about 15 minutes, or until cooked through. Remove and set aside.

For the rice, heat the ghee in a saucepan with a lid over a medium heat until melted. Add the cumin, star anise, peppercorns and black cardamom and heat for 30 seconds until the ghee is fragrant, or until the cumin begins to pop. Add the onions, garlic, ginger and green chillies and stir for 7–8 minutes, or until the onions are soft and light brown.

Add the drained rice and salt, then stir and mix for about 1 minute. Pour in 250–300ml/9–10 fl oz/1–1¼ cups water, or enough to cover the rice. Reduce the heat to low. Cover the pan with a tight-fitting lid and allow to cook for about 8–10 minutes, or until the rice is cooked. The liquid should be completely absorbed. If the rice isn't cooked, add a splash (or 1 tablespoon) of water, cover the pan and cook for a further 1-2 minutes.

Meanwhile, reheat the meatballs until piping hot.

To serve, sprinkle the meatballs with silver leaf. Put the cooked rice in a serving bowl, arrange the meatballs on top and garnish with the rose buds.

Meaty markets and weekdays bazaars
Lamb, beef and mutton

For a city devoted to its meat-centric cuisine, it's surprising that Tuesdays and Wednesdays are meatless days in Karachi. There's no slaughter, sale or consumption of meat on these days. Romantic stories are told about why this is – perhaps it was the court order of a Mughal Emperor named Akbar who married a Hindu-Rajput princess called Jodha. Since she was vegetarian, and he wanted to please her, he commanded that meatless days be observed. Perhaps not. Nowadays, the reasoning behind it seems more practical: such days preserve meat stocks, they allow butchers time off, and they keep the cost of meat in check. Nonetheless, they are difficult days for the typically carnivorous Pakistani.

My mother always ensures meat is available on meatless days, as my father really doesn't think a meal is complete without a meaty main course. It's an opinion I must have adopted at a young age. I have a vivid memory of being six years old and travelling on a ship with my family (my father was a navy captain) before being invited to a lavish Hindu vegetarian meal at a dock manager's humble home in Kandala, India. At the end of the meal, only an innocent child with a complete lack of tact could have asked: '*Where is dinner?*' On being told that this was it, I declared, '*But there is no dinner without meat!*' I was quickly presented with a wry smile from my father and a sweet treat to distract me from any further misdemeanour… The importance of meat to me has barely lessened since.

Red meat is the highlight of the Pakistani dining table: mutton is always the most popular, followed by beef and lamb, and they're always bought fresh from the bazaar or butcher. It may sound indulgent, but this insistence on meat is counteracted by a thrifty approach to cooking. In Pakistan, there's a strong belief that a meal should go further than just one day, and nothing should be scrapped – this is partly down to the large size of the families, low incomes and the high price of produce. But most of all, it's a spiritual belief that wasting food is unacceptable. In this chapter (as in others), I've added a couple of kitchen tips for making the most of every morsel – whether it's a chance to use bones as stock, or a fresh recipe for a portion of leftovers.

Much like meat dishes in Pakistan, the recipes here are often a heady fusion of layered spices, onions, garlic and fresh herbs, sometimes with the added sweetness of fruits and nuts. These rich, fragrant dishes are either slow-cooked, baked, barbecued or steamed to ensure well-cooked meat, rather than pink or rare lamb and beef. This is traditionally because meat does not keep in the Pakistani heat, so to be safe everything is cooked through – I've stuck to Pakistani cooking times in this chapter, but I leave it to your taste if you prefer a pinker meat.

The wonderful thing about Pakistani recipes is they always give you the option to use cheaper cuts of meat – high quality meat is usually extremely expensive in Pakistan, so slow-cooking, barbecueing and tenderising cheaper cuts give you a lot of flavour for your money. I've experimented successfully using cuts like featherblade or braising/chuck steak for slow-cooking and bavette for barbecuing – they work brilliantly.

Coal-smoked Bihari beef kebabs

Bihari kebabs found their way into Pakistani cuisine through the migration of Bihari Muslims from the north Indian state of Bihar when Pakistan formed in 1947. A firm favourite of mine, they can be made using the best beef fillet or chuck steak, tenderised using raw payaya, then infused with coal smoke using the method called 'dhuni' (see p22). They're eaten with rice and lentils by Biharis, and with paratha flatbreads by most other Pakistanis.

200g/7oz/scant 1 cup whole plain yogurt

1 red onion, ground into a paste

½ red onion, cut into half moons and fried until medium brown

1 tsp garam masala (see p26)

1 tsp ginger paste (traditionally Biharis don't use garlic in this recipe, but you can if you like add ½ tsp puréed garlic)

1 tbsp raw papaya paste (if you cannot find that, substitute with either 1 tbsp papaya powder or 1 tsp meat tenderiser)

1 tsp red chilli powder

1 tsp ground dry-roasted cumin seeds

1 tsp ground dry-roasted coriander (cilantro) seeds

salt, to taste

2–3 tbsp mustard seed oil

1 kg/2¼ lb chuck steak, cut into bite-sized cubes

To garnish

½ red onion, thinly sliced

handful of coriander (cilantro) leaves, chopped

1 lemon, cut into wedges

Equipment for smoking

quick-light coal – for smoking, you will also need a large saucepan with a tight-fitting lid, a small piece of bread, ghee (see p23) and matches

Preparation 25–30 minutes + 1 hour marinating | **Cooking** 30–40 minutes | **Serves** 10–12

Put the yogurt into a large bowl and add all the other ingredients, except the beef. Whisk together with a fork to combine, then add the meat and turn until it is coated in the yogurt mixture. Cover and allow to marinate in the fridge for 1 hour. Meanwhile, soak several wooden skewers in a bowl of water to prevent them burning during cooking.

Light a barbecue, if using, or preheat a griddle pan. Thread the meat on to the soaked skewers and either barbecue or cook on the griddle pan for about 10 minutes until cooked.

If you're not cooking on the barbecue, but you want to give it a smoky flavour, use the coal smoking (dhuni) method (see p22–23). Once the meat is cooked, put the skewers into a large saucepan with a lid, put the bread in the middle of the pan, then put the coal on top of the bread and pour 1 tablespoon ghee over the top. Heat the pan and as soon as it starts to smoke, cover with a lid and allow the smoke to infuse.

Serve with sliced onions and garnished with chopped coriander and lemon wedges.

Railway mutton curry ✓

Karachi Cantonment railway station is a legacy left by the British Raj and is now a protected heritage site which connects the whole of Pakistan through railway links built in the 1800s. At the bustling, noisy platforms, heavy with dust, one never misses the aroma of railway mutton curry bubbling away in a big cauldron. This thick, richly aromatic curry is alive with the scent of garam masala, coconut milk, curry leaves and tamarind, and is a nod to times gone by.

For the railway curry garam masala
1 tsp cumin seeds
1 tsp coriander (cilantro) seeds
2.5cm/1-inch cinnamon stick
6–7 cloves
4–5 green cardamom pods
1 tsp black peppercorns
1–2 dried red chillies

For the railway curry garam masala
500g/1lb 2oz mutton, with bones/
    lamb shoulder with bones, cut
    into medium pieces
600ml/1 pint/2½ cups water
4 tbsp vegetable oil
1 tbsp ghee (see p23)
2 red onions, cut into half moons,
    skins reserved for stock
1 tsp each of garlic purée and
    grated ginger
8–10 fresh curry leaves
salt, to taste
50g/1¾oz tamarind pulp (see p23)
    or 50g/1¾ oz tomato purée
50g/1¾oz/scant ¼ cup coconut milk

To garnish
handful of fresh tender coriander
    (cilantro) leaves with stems,
    chopped
1 green chilli, chopped

Preparation 15 minutes | **Cooking** 40–45 minutes | **Serves** 4–6

For the garam masala, grind all the spices in a spice grinder then set aside.

Put the meat into a large saucepan with the water and any onion or garlic skins and bring to the boil. Cook until the meat is tender, around 25 minutes, then remove the pan from the heat and take the meat out the pan and reserve. Set the stock aside.

Heat the oil and ghee in a large wok-style pan with a lid over a medium heat. Once hot, add the onions and cook for 5 minutes until golden brown. Add the garlic and ginger and cook for a further 2–3 minutes, or until the raw garlic smell disappears.

Add the curry leaves and allow to splutter, then add 1 tablespoon of the ground masala and stir-fry until everything is combined. Add a few splashes of the reserved stock if the spices start to burn. When the oil starts to rise, add the stock, meat and salt, then reduce the heat to low, partially cover with the lid and cook for 10–15 minutes until all the oil rises to the top of the curry. Add the tamarind or tomato purée and stir until well combined. Add the coconut milk and simmer over a very low heat for 5 minutes until hot.

Garnish with chopped green chillies and coriander and serve with naan, rice or even baked potatoes.

Kitchen secret

This dish aims to waste nothing, as the stock is used to flavour the curry. I recommend buying meat on the bone and adding the onion and garlic skins to the stock. If you are not a fan of mutton, use beef or goat instead.

Coal-smoked lamb keema

Keema (mince) is found in every home in Pakistan, from the most humble to the most extravagant. It is simple and affordable, and Pakistanis love to infuse it with whole garam masalas, top it with fresh vegetables and herbs, and create a kick with chillies to bring the simple mince to life. This is a recipe my mother and grandmother cooked at least twice a week, with my own contemporary twist. You can substitute lamb with mutton, beef or even chicken mince.

2 tbsp corn or sunflower oil
   (don't use olive)
1 red onion, chopped
1 tsp grated ginger
1 tsp crushed garlic paste
2 tomatoes, chopped
¼ tsp ground turmeric
½ tsp red chilli powder
½ tsp ground coriander
   (cilantro) seeds
½ tsp ground cumin seeds
1 tsp salt
500g/1lb 2oz lamb mince (ground
   lamb)
1 tsp dried methi (fenugreek) leaves

For the whole garam masalas
5–6 black peppercorns
6 cloves
1 black cardamom pod
½ tsp cumin seeds
1 star anise
1 bay leaf
2.5-cm/1-inch cinnamon stick
1 tsp coriander (cilantro) seeds

To garnish
chopped coriander (cilantro)
chopped cherry tomatoes (or
   seasonal tomatoes of any kind)
chopped spring onions (scalllions)
   or seasonal leeks softened in
   a little butter)
lemon juice
ginger, peeled and cut into julienne
garam masala (see p26)

Preparation 10 minutes | **Cooking** 25–30 minutes | **Serves** 4–5

Heat the oil in a sauté saucepan over a medium heat. When hot, add the whole garam masalas and allow to splutter for 30 seconds. Once the garam masalas are fragrant, add the onions and fry until light brown. Add the ginger and garlic and cook for 1–2 minutes, or until the raw smell disappears.

Add the chopped tomatoes and a splash of water and cook for 7–8 minutes until the tomatoes are soft and the oil rises to the top. Add all the ground spices and salt, then add the meat and cook for a further 7–8 minutes, stirring constantly until all the moisture has evaporated.

Add the dried methi leaves, then cover the pan and cook over a medium-low heat for 5–7 minutes until the water evaporates and meat is cooked through, dark brown and dry.

To add a smoky flavour, use the dhuni technique on p22–3. Once ready to serve, heat until piping hot and top with all the garnishes. Serve with daal and plain basmati rice or chapati flatbread.

Kitchen secret

If you have leftover keema, use it to make my mother's keema cutlets for a quick lunch or snack. You'll need about 100g/3½ oz leftover keema. Peel and boil 3 Maris Piper potatoes, mash with 1 tablespoon milk, a knob of butter and a little salt to taste. Put 50g/2oz/1 cup breadcrumbs in a bowl, and 1 beaten egg in another. Scoop up about 2 tablespoons mash, flatten it in your hand, then place about 2–3 teaspoons of keema in the middle. Top it with 1 tablespoon mash to form a roughly shaped ball. Flatten gently into a burger bun shape, then dip in the egg, and roll in the breadcrumbs to coat. Shallow-fry until light brown on both sides then drain on kitchen paper.

Peshawari namkeen gosht
Salted meat curry

A dish from Peshawar in north Pakistan, namkeen gosht has a clean, fresh flavour that's down to Peshawaris preferring very little spice and chilli in their robust meat dishes. The flavour comes from the meat fat (consumed for its warming properties in cold, harsh winters). The authentic method of cooking would be on a coal fire in a 'handi' (clay pot) or 'pateli' (a stainless steel cooking pot), which adds a smoky flavour. This is quite a dry stir-fry, rather than a curry-based dish.

1 kg/2¼lb fatty mutton pieces on the bone, all fat removed to use as cooking fat, or use 3 tbsp vegetable oil
2 tomatoes, finely chopped
2 tsp ground Himalayan pink salt
½ tsp crushed garlic
1cm/½-inch piece ginger, peeled and cut into julienne
1 green chilli, chopped
½ tsp ground black pepper
1 lime, cut into half

Preparation 10 minutes | **Cooking** 40–45 minutes | **Serves** 4–6

Place a wok-style pan over a medium heat, add the reserved fat from the mutton and allow to melt slowly, adding a little oil to help the melting process. Add all the meat, cover the pan and reduce the heat to medium low and cook for about 15 minutes, stirring occasionally.

Uncover and cook, stirring constantly until nearly all the moisture has evaporated. Add the tomatoes, salt and garlic and stir-fry for 10–15 minutes until the tomato is cooked through and dry.

Add the ginger julienne, green chilli, black pepper and a squeeze of lime before serving.

Kitchen secret
Try using any animal fat (such as beef dripping) that is easily available instead of oil or ghee in this recipe for an authentic flavour.

Punjabi aloo gosht
Mutton and potato curry

My mother's family come from Pakistani Punjab, where flavours are simple and no meat stew is cooked without a vegetable. This is a land of agriculture and seasonal produce, and the simplicity of this dish is not a failing, but a celebration of what the land provides (without it being masked by spice). Aloo gosht is so revered in Punjab that poetry has been written about it. This recipe has been passed on by my mother's cousin Tanveer Khala and has graced many family meals.

50ml/2 fl oz/ scant ¼ cup vegetable oil
1 large red onion, finely chopped
1cm/½-inch piece ginger, peeled and grated
2 garlic cloves, minced
1 kg/2¼lb mutton with bone, cut into 5–6cm/2–2.5-inch chunks
1–2 tsp salt
½ tsp ground turmeric
1 tsp plain paprika (not smoked)
1 tsp red chilli powder
250–450ml/9–16 fl oz/1–2 cups water
3–4 tbsp vegetable oil
2 medium tomatoes, finely chopped
1 tsp dry-roasted and ground coriander (cilantro) seeds
500g/1lb 2oz Maris Piper potatoes, peeled and quartered

To garnish
1 tsp garam masala (see p26)
2 tbsp chopped coriander (cilantro) leaves
2 green chillies, finely chopped

Preparation 20 minutes | **Cooking** 65–70 minutes | **Serves** 4–6

Heat the oil in a large saucepan with a lid over a medium heat. When hot, add the onions, ginger and garlic and cook for 7–8 minutes until the onions are light brown. Add the mutton pieces, salt, turmeric, paprika and red chilli powder then add 150ml/5 fl oz/⅔ cup water and reduce the heat to medium low. Cover the pan with the lid and cook for about 15–20 minutes until the mutton is tender and the curry is reddish brown, checking the water has not dried up – if it does add about 20ml/¾ fl oz/4 teaspoons water to ensure that the mutton is just covered.

Increase the heat to medium high, add the vegetable oil, tomatoes and ground coriander seeds. Stir-fry to allow the oil in the pan to cook through the tomatoes and create a thick red sauce with oil separating and rising to the surface of the curry.

Add the potatoes and 200–300ml/7–10 fl oz/scant 1–1¼ cups water, depending on how watery you prefer the curry (traditionally it is quite watery), then reduce the heat to medium-low and continue to cook for 10–15 minutes until the potatoes are tender. The curry should be red with oil rising to the surface but watery. If this has not happened yet, keep the saucepan on a very low heat for a further 5–10 minutes, but make sure not to overcook the potatoes.

Turn off the heat, cover with the lid and let the curry simmer in its own heat for about 10 minutes before serving. When ready to serve, transfer to a serving dish and garnish with garam masala, chopped coriander and chopped green chillies. This is best served with plain basmati rice or naan bread.

Attock chapli kebab

Mince beef flat kebab with pomegranate chutney

This recipe comes from one of my oldest friends Moneeza and is inspired by her fondest food memory: travelling by a horse-drawn 'tanga' (carriage) through the mustard fields of Punjab to her home in Attock where she would be greeted with the intoxicating aromas of her mother's sizzling chapli kebabs. These flattened kebabs are large – the size of a 'chapal' (slipper) – and come wrapped in newspaper topped with spring onions and garlicky pomegranate chutney.

1kg/2¼lb fine beef mince (ground beef) with fat

1 red onion, very finely chopped

4 spring onions (scallions), very finely chopped

1–2 green chillies, very finely chopped

2 handfuls of finely chopped coriander (cilantro)

1 large tomato, finely chopped

1 tbsp dry-roasted coriander (cilantro) seeds, ground in a mortar and pestle

2.5cm/1-inch piece ginger, peeled and grated on a grater (like a Microplane)

2 tbsp ground anardana (dried pomegranate)

1½ tbsp cornmeal flour or fine polenta (or use gram flour)

salt, to taste

1 egg

3–5 tbsp vegetable oil

To garnish

3–5 red radishes, chopped

1 tomato, sliced

2 spring onions (scallions), chopped

1 lime

Preparation 15 minutes + overnight marinating | **Cooking** 15–20 minutes | **Serves** 6

Mix all the ingredients, except the oil, together in a large bowl. Begin kneading and squeezing the mixture together like you would a dough. The more you knead and squeeze everything together by hand, the less chance it will break when frying. Continue kneading and squeezing the mixture until it feels sticky then cover with clingfilm and allow to rest in the fridge overnight.

Before frying allow the mixture to come to room temperature first. Using your hands, take about 3 heaped tablespoons of the mixture and shape into a flat oblong kebab about 5mm/¼ inch thick and about 13cm/5 inches wide (at the greatest width).

Using a tawa, pancake pan, griddle or frying pan, heat a 1 teaspoon oil for each kebab. Add 2–3 kebabs at a time and cook on one side. If the kebab is very thin, it will take about 3–5 minutes. Remove from the pan and repeat with the remaining kebabs.

To serve, place a hot kebab on top of a naan (see p58), add the radish, tomato, spring onion, a squeeze of lime and a little of the pomegranate chutney below.

Kitchen secret

For the pomegranate chutney, mix 3 tablespoons dried and ground anardana (dried pomegranate) with 1 finely chopped green chilli, 1 crushed garlic clove, a large handful of chopped coriander and 10 chopped mint leaves. Bash it all up in a mortar and pestle and serve with chapli kebabs (see above).

Lamb karhai with fennel and coriander

This 'karhai' (a wok-like pan) dish is a staple on the weekday dining table. It's a quick and easy recipe, compared to many of Pakistan's slow-cooked meat dishes, and is essentially a one-pot meal which requires very little fuss. As with a stir fry, you need to stand by your dish while all the spices infuse and cook with the meat, and then finish off with a bit of dum (steam) cooking.

600g/1¼ lb boneless lamb or
    mutton pieces
5 tomatoes, chopped (reserve 1
    tomato for later)
½ tsp garlic paste
½ tsp ginger paste
1 tbsp ghee (see p23)
2 tbsp vegetable oil
1 tsp cumin seeds
1 tsp fennel seeds
1cm/½-inch piece ginger, peeled
    and finely chopped
1–2 medium onions, chopped
1–2 garlic cloves, roughly chopped
¼ tsp ground turmeric
salt, to taste
1 tsp each of dried red chilli and
    coriander (cilantro) seeds ground
    together

To garnish
handful of coriander (cilantro) leaves,
    chopped
10 mint leaves, chopped
1–3 green chillies, finely chopped

Preparation 20 minutes | **Cooking** 45 minutes | **Serves** 4–5

Place the lamb with 4 of the chopped tomatoes in a dry pan and add the ginger and garlic pastes. Cook for about 20–25 minutes until all the water from the meat and tomatoes runs dry. Remove the meat from the pan and set aside.

Add a combination of ghee and oil to the same pan and heat over a medium heat until hot. Add the cumin and fennel and fry for 1 minute, or until they start to splutter. Add the chopped ginger, onion, garlic, turmeric and salt and cook for about 30 seconds, or until the raw garlic smell disappears. Add the pre-cooked meat to the pan and fry for a further 1 minute. Add the remaining tomatoes and stir-fry for about 15 minutes, or until the meat is dry, then add the ground coriander and red chilli powder and stir-fry briefly until the spices are mixed in.

To serve, top with coriander leaves, mint and green chilli. It is delicious eaten with freshly baked naans (see p58) or even simple boiled basmati rice and accompanied with a simple daal (see p143).

Rose garam masala mutton chops

If there is one aroma that transports me back to Pakistan, it would be rose petals. In Pakistan we grow a variety of rose, or rather it grows on its own, called 'desi gulab' (rose of the land). There is none like it in the world: its depth of intense fragrance and deep purple-red hue are incomparable. They are used for every occasion, be it happy or sad, and I love using flowers alongside spice as they set each other off in a magical and exotic way.

Preparation 10 minutes + 1 hour marinating | **Cooking** 20 minutes | **Serves** 6

Grind all the spices for the garam masala in a spice grinder and set aside. Mix all the ingredients together, except the meat, in a large bowl. Add most of the garam masala, mix, then add the mutton chops. Cover and allow to marinate in the fridge overnight.

Preheat a griddle pan or light a barbecue. Remove the chops from the marinade and grill for 20 minutes, or until tender. Serve sprinkled with the remaining garam masala and garnishes.

300g/10½oz/1¼ cups whole plain
    yogurt, whipped
2 tbsp double (heavy) cream
1 tsp ginger paste
2–4 wild garlic flowers, torn or
    1 garlic clove, puréed
1 red onion, cut into half moons,
    then fried until light brown
    and ground into a paste
juice of ½ lime
salt, to taste
6 meaty mutton chops

For the rose petal garam masala
1½ tbsp dried edible rose petals
1 star anise
2.5cm/1-inch cinnamon stick
½ tsp cumin seeds
6 cloves
5 green cardamom pods
1 long dried red chilli

To garnish
lemon slices
1 tbsp edible rose petals
1 green chilli, chopped
handful of pomegranate seeds

Hunter beef
Salted, slow-cooked meat

This is a true Pakistani classic. It's a salt-cured and spiced cut of beef, infused with cinnamon, cardamom, black pepper and jaggery, and marinated for up to five days before being boiled gently until cooked. There is nothing that can compare to its succulent texture, subtle spicing and versatility of use – the best way to describe it is as a cross between corned beef and salt beef. Use it in sandwiches with mustard and salad.

3 tsp black peppercorns
5cm/2-inch cinnamon stick
½ tsp cloves
3 tbsp jaggery or muscovado sugar
1 tbsp cumin seeds
juice of 2 lemons
3 tsp salt
1½ tbsp saltpetre or curing salts
1 kg/2¼ lb beef brisket
500ml/17 fl oz/2 cups water

For the spicy mustard
2 tbsp Dijon mustard
1 tsp red chilli flakes,
    more to garnish
½ tsp sea salt
juice of ½ a lime

Preparation 30 minutes + 4–5 days curing | **Cooking** 1–1 hour 10 minutes | **Serves** 6–8

Grind together the black peppercorns, cinnamon, cloves, jaggery and cumin in a spice grinder then put into a bowl and mix with the lemon juice, salt and saltpetre to make a marinade. Pierce the beef all over with a skewer then rub the marinade all over the beef. Place in a dish, cover with foil and chill in the fridge for a minimum of 4 days and a maximum of 5 days piercing the beef daily.

On the fifth day, remove the beef and tie it up with kitchen string over and across to secure. Put the beef into a large saucepan with a lid over a medium heat and top it up with the measured water along with any leftover marinade. Partially cover the pan with the lid, reduce the heat to low and cook the beef for 1–1 hour and 10 minutes, or until tender. The water should dry up in the pan.

Once the beef is cooked, allow to cool, then cut into slices and serve either on its own as a cold meat or pull the meat into shreds and mix with mayonnaise and use as a sandwich filling. You can also serve with the spicy mustard sauce. Combine all the ingredients for the sauce, stir well. Serve in a bowl sprinkled with chilli flakes.

The cooked beef can last in the fridge for up to 10 days and is best enjoyed at room temperature.

Birds from the Empress
Chicken and other birds

As a child I loved going with my mother and grandmother to the bustling Empress market in Karachi. It was full of smells (both pleasant and less so), suffocating in its humidity and loud with the call of stallholders shouting out their prices and young boys offering to carry your shopping in exchange for a rupee. As you walked from the cooked food and vegetable stalls toward the meat market, the aromas of chicken tikkas grilling on the barbecue and earthy vegetables would be replaced by the smell of live chickens and raw meat.

We'd always find our regular butcher sitting beside what looked like a bottomless pit (where he'd throw feathers and off cuts) with a sharp knife by the side of his overused butcher's block. Still today, the chickens are held in pens and shoppers pick a bird before the butcher weighs it on an old fashioned scale. He then offers the 'kalma' (the prayer just before slaughtering), chops its head off, plucks the bird clean, pops it in a plastic bag (still warm from its last breath) and you're on your way. Seeing and understanding this process is how I grew up – and now I have a relaxed acceptance of the journey my food takes before it lands on my plate. And I'm happy to know that things haven't changed for today's children in my home country.

In Pakistan, chicken is the cheapest form of meat and also the most popular for barbecuing. It ranges from Lahori chargha – a whole chicken marinated in as many as 24 different spices, steam-cooked then flash-fried for crispiness – to the traditional Baluchi sajji: a whole chicken marinated in simple spices, slow-roasted using a long skewer on a coal spit roast, and served with a sprinkling of chaat masala. But by far the most popular Pakistani chicken meal is the invention of Bundu Khan (a popular barbecue chain), which revolutionised barbecue culture in Pakistan – spicy chicken tikkas. The recipes in this chapter highlight my interpretation of some of these distinctly Pakistani dishes that are found both on street corners and in the home.

Baluchi-style chicken sajji

Roast chicken with fennel and mango powder

Sajji is the native dish of the province of Baluchistan – here, food is simple and cooking techniques rather rustic. Dishes usually feature spit-roasted meat or poultry, and sajji is traditionally a large leg of lamb, stuffed with pulao rice and slow-cooked over coals. The chicken version is also popular, and all over Pakistan large open-air ovens cook chickens to be topped with spicy sajji masala. My contemporary take on this dish can be an alternative to a traditional Sunday roast.

1.5kg/3¼lb whole chicken, with skin
½ tsp salt
½ tsp ground black pepper
4 garlic cloves, crushed
2 tbsp vegetable oil
2 tbsp sajji masala (you can substitute the above sajji masala with shop-bought chaat masala available in most South Asian grocery stores)
juice of 1 lemon

Preparation 15 minutes | **Cooking** 45–60 minutes | **Serves** 4–6

Rub the whole chicken with the salt, pepper and crushed garlic. Heat a large saucepan, big enough to hold the chicken, add the oil and the chicken and cook until the chicken is sealed and lightly browned all over. Turn the heat off and allow the chicken to cool.

Preheat the oven to 190°C/375°F/gas mark 5. Put the chicken into a roasting tin and loosely cover with foil. Roast in the oven, basting the chicken with the oil until it is cooked through, the top is golden and the juices run clear when the thickest part of the meat is pierced with a skewer.

Allow the chicken to rest for 5 minutes then cut into quarters. Sprinkle the ground sajji and lemon juice over the chicken and serve with Mummy's biryani-style saffron rice (see p69).

Kitchen secret

A weekend chicken sajji carcass can be used to make a stock base for a soup. Boil in water with star anise, cinnamon, ginger and coriander stalks. Top the stock with shredded leftover chicken, a sprinkle of chaat masala (see p26) and a splash of lime juice to complete the hearty soup. If you have leftover chicken sajji pieces, toss in a temper (see p22) infused with cumin, mustard seeds and mixed peppers. Once reheated, garnish with chopped coriander and green chillies, and a sprinkle of garam masala (see p26).

Masaledar batair
Spicy stir-fried quails

Pakistan has a rich game culture and 'shirkar' (hunting) is something enjoyed by many people in the northern areas of the country in particular. Deer, as well as partridge, quail and other small birds, are popular and are cooked simply and quickly. This is a quick and easy recipe for batair (quail) and can be cooked on an open fire or at home on the hob. The key with quail is to cook the sauce first and then quickly stir-fry the birds to avoid overcooking.

3–4 tbsp corn or sunflower oil
3–4 cloves
2.5cm/1-inch cinnamon stick
1 black cardamom pod
1 bay leaf
1 tsp cumin seeds
1 large red onion, cut into rings
½ tsp grated ginger
1 garlic clove, crushed
4 tomatoes, roughly chopped
salt, to taste
¼ tsp ground turmeric
¾ tsp red chilli powder
4 quails

To garnish
fresh tender coriander (cilantro)
    with stems, chopped

Preparation 15 minutes | **Cooking** 25 minutes | **Serves** 4

Heat the oil in a wok-style pan over a medium heat. When hot, add the cloves, cinnamon, black cardamom, bay leaf and cumin seeds and fry for 30 seconds, or until they start to splutter. Add the onion and cook for 3–4 minutes until light brown, then add the ginger and garlic and stir-fry for a further 2–3 minutes, or until the raw smell of the garlic and ginger disappears.

Add about half the tomatoes, salt, turmeric and red chilli powder to the pan and stir-fry for 2 minutes until soft. Add the quails and fry over a high heat for 6–7 minutes, then add the remaining tomatoes and stir-fry for another 5–6 minutes until the quails are cooked. The sauce should be quite dry and thick. If it sticks to the base of the pan, stir in a few splashes of water.

Once cooked, reduce the heat to really low, cover the pan and let the quails cook in their own steam for a minute or two.

Garnish with coriander and serve hot with naan (see p58), rice and a vegetable accompaniment.

Karhai ginger chicken

On the days I was greeted with the hot citrus tang of fresh ginger from my grandmother's garden as it was sliced artfully into julienne pieces, I knew I was getting Pakistani-style ginger chicken for supper. This is a dish that is found in every restaurant and home in Pakistan and is simple and quick to make, with bursts of raw ginger added at the end for a fresh finish. Serve with a daal and rice – and you can substitute chicken with boneless duck or turkey for a fuller flavour.

2 tbsp vegetable oil
I tsp cumin seeds
I tsp each of garlic purée and
    grated ginger
200g/7oz chicken breast cut into
    5cm/2-inch chunks
2 large tomatoes, finely chopped
I tbsp tomato purée
2 tbsp plain yogurt
½ tsp red chilli powder
½ tsp freshly ground black pepper
¼ tsp ground turmeric
salt, to taste
I tbsp unsalted butter

To garnish
5cm/2-inch piece ginger, peeled
    and cut into julienne
handful of coriander (cilantro)
    leaves, chopped
2 green chillies, finely chopped
10 mint leaves, chopped

Preparation 10 minutes | **Cooking** 25–30 minutes | **Serves** 4

Heat the oil in wok-style pan over a medium heat. When hot, add the cumin and allow to splutter for 30 seconds. Add the garlic purée and grated ginger and fry for a further 30 seconds, or until the raw smell of garlic disappears.

Add the chicken to the pan and fry until it is sealed all over. Add the tomatoes and cook for 5–7 minutes until softened, then add the tomato purée and the yogurt and cook for 8–10 minutes, or until the oil starts to separate. Add the red chilli powder, black pepper, turmeric and salt and cook for a further 5–7 minutes until the chicken is done. Add the butter before turning off the heat and letting the butter melt.

Before serving, add the julienned ginger, coriander, green chillies and mint, and stir through.

Karachi-style chicken tikka

On the bone with red chilli masala

As night descends on Karachi, the air is weighty with the day's humid heat and wafts of coal smoke tempting anyone nearby with an aroma of red chillies and spices. Who can resist a fresh, hot chicken tikka? These are perfect with puri breads and green chutney (p101).

Preparation 10 minutes + 50 minutes soaking & marinating | **Cooking** 25 minutes | **Serves** 4

5–6 dried red chillies

1½ tsp salt

1 tsp each of garlic purée and grated ginger

juice of 1 lime

½ tsp freshly ground pepper

½ tsp ground turmeric

1 tbsp brown sugar

½ dry-roasted coriander seeds

½ tbsp tamarind paste (or homemade pulp, see p23)

1 tsp dry-roasted cumin seeds

1 tbsp sunflower or corn oil

1 whole chicken, without skin, quartered

Soak the chillies in warm water for 20 minutes, then drain. In a mortar and pestle, grind the red chillies with the salt. Add the remaining ingredients, except the chicken, and grind to make a marinade. Put the marinade in a bowl, add the chicken and turn until the chicken is coated. Cover and marinate in the fridge for 30 minutes, or overnight.

Light a barbecue or preheat a griddle pan. Remove the chicken from the marinade and cook for 20–25 minutes (you can do this on skewers if you like, or until the chicken is cooked through then serve.

Lahori chargha

Steamed and flash-fried whole chicken with an aromatic spice blend

Walking along food streets in Lahore, my attention was always drawn to the vibrant orange-coloured chickens stacked up on large stainless-steel platters. Chargha is a whole chicken marinated overnight, steamed and then flash-fried to give it a caramelised flavour and crispy skin.

Preparation 10 minutes + 1 hour marinating | **Cooking** 45–55 minutes | **Serves** 4–6

1 kg/2¼ lb whole chicken, skinned

2 large tbsp chargha masala (see p27)

100g/3½oz/scant ½ cup Greek yogurt

1 tsp each grated ginger and crushed garlic

1 tbsp white wine vinegar

¼ tsp red food colour (optional)

salt, to taste

sunflower oil, for frying

handful of coriander (cilantro) leaves, chopped

1 lemon

Score the chicken all over with a sharp knife. Mix the yogurt, ginger, garlic, vinegar, red food colour, if using, and salt together in a large bowl until well combined. Add the ground chargha masala then add the chicken and turn until the chicken is coated. Cover with clingfilm and allow to marinate in the fridge for 1 hour, or overnight.

When ready to cook, remove the chicken from the marinade and cook in a steamer for 40–45 minutes, or until the juices run clear when the thickest part of the meat is pierced with a skewer.

Just before serving, heat about 4 tablespoons of oil in a wok and flash-fry the steamed chicken for a few minutes until the outside is caramelised all over.

Sprinkle with coriander, any leftover spice blend and lemon juice then serve.

Chicken makhani handi

With coconut milk and fenugreek

Pottery stalls selling earthenware line many pavements in Pakistan. Unglazed terracotta pots are great for making firni (ground rice pudding, p190) as the rice takes on some of the raw earthy essence of the pot it's cooked in. This dish is made in a 'handi' – a small clay cooking pot that's often better known as 'balti', and said to have its roots in Baltistan, in north Pakistan. If you don't have a handi or a balti dish (or an open fire!), make this in a wok on a high heat.

3 tbsp sunflower or corn oil

I tsp each of coriander (cilantro) and cumin seeds

I large red onion, finely chopped

I tsp each of grated ginger and crushed garlic

2 tomatoes, roughly chopped

250g/9oz skinless, boneless chicken breast or thigh, cut into 2.5cm/ I-inch pieces

I tsp ground garam masala (see p26)

I tsp sea salt

I tsp red chilli powder

½ tsp freshly ground black pepper

I tsp dried methi (fenugreek) leaves

50g/1¾ oz/scant ¼ cup Greek yogurt

I tbsp coconut milk powder or coconut cream

I tbsp double (heavy) cream

To garnish

handful of coriander (cilantro) leaves

2 green chillies, finely chopped

I tbsp gingee, peeled and cut into julienne

Preparation I5 minutes | **Cooking** 30 minutes | **Serves** 4–6

Heat the oil in a wok, karhai, handi or balti pan over a medium heat. When hot, add the coriander and cumin seeds and fry for 30 seconds, or until they start to pop. Add the onion and stir-fry for 8–10 minutes until brown.

Add the ginger and garlic and fry until the raw smell of the garlic disappears. Add the tomatoes and cook for 8–10 minutes until soft and the oil starts to rise to the top. You may need to add a splash of water to prevent the tomatoes burning.

Add the chicken, garam masala, salt and red chilli and stir-fry for I5 minutes until the chicken is half cooked. Add the dried methi and yogurt and cook for 5–7 minutes.

Once the chicken is done, add the coconut powder and stir through. Add the cream and heat through. Serve garnished with chopped coriander, green chillies and ginger.

Kitchen secret

If you are lactose intolerant, try using soya cream, coconut yogurt or almond milk instead of the fresh cream.

Lahori murgh cholay

Chickpea and chicken curry

This wonderful curry can be eaten with tandoori naans for a satisfying breakfast or simple lunch. Soaking and boiling dried chickpeas is well worth the trouble for this dish – you can also add half-boiled eggs to the curry at the end of the cooking time to make it even more filling.

500g/1lb 2oz dried chickpeas
1 tbsp masoor daal
½ tsp bicarbonate of soda (baking soda)
50ml/2 fl oz/scant ¼ cup vegetable oil
1 heaped tsp cumin seeds
1 tsp coriander (cilantro) seeds
2.5cm/1-inch cinnamon stick
1 small red onion, finely chopped
1 tsp each of grated ginger and crushed garlic
1kg/2¼lb chicken, skinned and cut into 4 pieces
1 tsp red chilli powder
½ tsp ground turmeric
salt, to taste
1 tsp garam masala (see p26)
500ml/17 fl oz/2 cups water

To garnish
ginger, peeled and cut into julienne
coriander (cilantro) leaves, chopped
2 hard-boiled eggs, halved (optional)

Preparation 30 minutes + overnight soaking | **Cooking** 55 minutes–1 hour | **Serves** 6

Soak the chickpeas overnight in a bowl of water. The next day, put the chickpeas, masoor daal and bicarbonate of soda into a large saucepan with enough water to cover and bring to the boil. Cook until the chickpeas are soft (see kitchen secret, below), then drain and set aside.

Heat the oil in a saucepan with a lid over a medium heat. When hot, add the cumin, coriander and cinnamon and fry until the spices splutter. Add the onions, ginger and garlic and fry for 8–10 minutes until golden. Add the chicken and cook for 15–20 minutes until the chicken is browned and all the liquid dries up. Add the chilli powder, turmeric, salt and garam masala and continue frying until the spices begin to stick to the base of the pan.

Add the measured water, bring to the boil, then add the chickpeas and masoor daal and stir. Cover the pan with the lid, turn the heat to medium low and cook for 30 minutes, or until the chicken is cooked through. You may need to add more water as it cooks to ensure that you are left with a substantial curry. Once the oil rises to the top, turn off the heat, garnish with ginger julienne, coriander and eggs and serve hot with naan (see p58).

Kitchen secret

To use dried chickpeas, soak them in enough water to cover the chickpeas comfortably (some of the water will be absorbed, and you want them to remain covered all night) with ½ teaspoon bicarbonate of soda. The next day, boil the chickpeas using the same water plus more to cover them well until soft, about 25–30 minutes. Rinse the chickpeas and drain thoroughly before adding to curries.

Chicken salan

On-the-bone chicken curry

Salan means a liquid-based stew, and the closest description in English would be a thin curry. An everyday staple, chicken salan is classically made using chicken on the bone alongside onion, ginger and garlic with tomatoes and a simple combination of spice. Feel free to experiment with different spice combinations to make this dish your own. It's best served with an accompaniment of daal, rice and a vegetable dish.

3–4 tbsp corn oil
2 red onions, roughly chopped
1-cm/½-inch piece ginger, peeled and grated
1 garlic clove, crushed
400g/14oz can chopped tomatoes or 5 tomatoes, chopped
1 tsp tomato purée (optional)
salt, to taste
1 tsp red chilli powder (reduce if required)
¼ ground turmeric
1 kg/2¼ lb chicken with bones (ask butcher to cut a whole skinned chicken into 16 pieces with bone or use about 500g/1lb 2oz deboned thighs or chicken breast pieces (2.5–5cm/1–2 inches large)
100ml/3½ fl oz/½ cup water, plus 5–8 tbsp

For the ground spices
1 tsp cumin seeds
3–4 green cardamom pods
1 bay leaf
1 tsp coriander (cilantro) seeds

To garnish
handful of tender fresh coriander (cilantro) with stems, chopped
2 green chillies, finely chopped

Preparation 15 minutes | **Cooking** 45–55 minutes | **Serves** 4–6

For the ground spices, grind all the spices together then set aside. Heat the oil in a heavy-based saucepan over a medium heat. When hot, add the onions and cook for 8–10 minutes until golden. Add the ginger and garlic and cook for 30 seconds or so until the raw smell disappears. Add the ground spices, reserving a teaspoon of the spices to garnish. Now cook for about 10–15 minutes until everything is caramelised. The onions will start to darken, and the garlic and ginger will also begin to caramelise. This is what you need for an intensely coloured base.

Add the tomatoes, tomato purée, salt, chilli and turmeric then turn the heat to medium and bhuno (stir-fry) this mixture. If the tomatoes start to splutter a lot reduce the heat slightly. Cook for about 20 minutes until you are left with a thick, rich sauce.

Turn off the heat, let the tomato mixture cool, then blitz in a blender until smooth. Add 5–8 tablespoons water to make sure it is not too thick – it should be the consistency of a thick jam. Return to the pan, add the chicken pieces and 50ml/2 fl oz/scant ¼ cup of the water and increase the heat to medium-high. Bhuno (stir-fry) the chicken until you start to see the oil separating from the sauce, about 15 minutes of vigorous stirring.

Reduce the heat to low, add about another 50ml/2 fl oz/scant ¼ cup water, cover and cook until the oil floats on top of the curry sauce and the chicken is cooked through.

Garnish with chopped coriander, chillies and a sprinkling of the spice blend. Serve with basmati rice, chapati and a salad such as crispy chapati kachumber salad (see p136).

Hara masala turkey keema

With coriander, mint and green chilli

You can combine this spicy, herb-filled, aromatic mince stir-fry with naan for a reviving breakfast or quick lunch. You can even have it as a simple dinner if you add a vegetable dish or a pickle, and of course some bread or rice. Use chicken mince if turkey doesn't appeal.

2 tsp ghee (see p23)
1 tsp sunflower oil
1 tsp cumin seeds
1 tsp black peppercorns
1 tsp coriander (cilantro) seeds
1cm/½-inch cinnamon stick
1 red onion, finely chopped
1 tsp grated ginger
½ tsp crushed garlic
½ tsp red chilli powder
400g/14oz turkey mince
  (ground turkey)
1 tsp dried methi (fenugreek) leaves
salt, to taste

To garnish
½ bunch of coriander (cilantro)
  leaves, very finely chopped
  with stems
15 mint leaves, finely chopped
2 green chillies, finely chopped

Preparation 10 minutes | **Cooking** 20 minutes | **Serves** 4

Heat the ghee and oil together in a shallow saucepan or sauté pan with a lid over a medium heat. When hot, add the cumin, black peppercorns, coriander seeds and cinnamon and fry for 30 seconds or so until they start to splutter. Add the onion, ginger and garlic and cook for 5–7 minutes until the onions are light brown around the edges and the raw smell of ginger and garlic disappears.

Add the red chilli powder and turkey mince and bhuno (stir-fry) for 10–15 minutes until all the water evaporates and the mince is cooked through. Add the methi leaves, reduce the heat to low, cover with a lid and allow to cook in its own steam for about 2 minutes. Season with salt just before turning off the heat.

Garnish with the chopped coriander leaves, mint leaves and green chilli and serve hot with naan (see p58) or rice and a daal (see p143). This is also a great breakfast with puris (see p61) and spicy scrambled eggs (see p33).

Sailing the seas
Seafood and fish

The Arabian Sea breeze carries with it the warm, salty promise of my hometown, Karachi. Pakistan's coastline is unexplored by most, leaving an absence in many minds of its captivating beauty and abundant seafood. Karachi is the largest Pakistani port and is a haven of edible treasures, from both the briny sea water and the fresh Indus River which flows into it.

My early years were not conventional. I spent much of my childhood growing up on a cargo vessel captained by my father. My passion for the sea, for food and for cooking all began there. Food was my main connection to reality and home in this surreal life. My mother never stopped cooking onboard, making everything from cakes to seafood biryani, all in one electric frying pan. Being on a boat for months on end, there was little understanding of the provenance of food, but certain moments would bring it to life. I remember catching the flying fish that leapt on to the ship's lower deck, quickly coating them in salt and crushed red chillies, and flash frying them... a pure flavour of the ocean.

Most coastal-living Pakistanis buy seafood either fresh from the bazaar (where fisherman sell their catch in the early hours), or from a fisherman's home-delivery service. That might sound like a luxury, but it's the best and most cost-effective way to get the finest seafood. Large jute baskets filled with ice are topped with fresh, seasonal fish, gutted and prepared to personal liking, then delivered to your house directly.

The Arabian Sea is criss-crossed with ancient trade routes that brought invaders, religion and travellers over many centuries to Pakistan. It's no wonder the country's coast has such an eclectic cuisine. My seafood recipes are not only inspired by the bounty of fresh lobsters, king prawns and other seasonal catch, but the diverse communities who cooked them.

Spicy crabs

As a teenager I'd take weekend trips to Kemari jetty for a night-crabbing cruise with friends. Once out of the harbour, we would throw lines in and 'fish' our crabs for dinner. The boatmen then served up a feast of fresh 'tawa' (pan) cooked crabs with red chilli masala mopped up with naans. The rustic presentation and simplicity of the spices is deeply etched in my mind, and though the boatmen would never share their recipe, I have created this from memory.

2 bay leaves
2–3 dried red chillies
1 tsp each dry-roasted cumin
   and coriander (cilantro) seeds
3–4 tbsp sunflower oil
2 garlic cloves, crushed
juice of 1 lemon
salt, to taste
½ tsp Kashmiri chilli powder
1 crab, humanely killed by your
   fishmonger, steamed and
   claws detached

To garnish
lemon wedges
fresh tender coriander (cilantro)
   leaves with stems, chopped

Preparation 15 minutes | **Cooking** 2–4 minutes | **Serves** 2–4

First make the ground spice blend by grinding the bay leaves and red chillies with the cumin and coriander seeds in a spice grinder or mortar and pestle until finely ground.

Heat the oil in a sauté pan with a lid over a medium heat. When hot, add the garlic and stir-fry for 2–4 minutes until light brown. Add the ground spice blend with the lemon juice and stir-fry for 2 minutes until the oil begins to rise to the top. Don't let the garlic and spices burn – you may need to add a few splashes of water to prevent this from happening.

Add salt to taste and the Kashmiri chilli powder and cook for a further 2–3 minutes. Add the steamed crab and stir through. Cover with the lid, reduce the heat to the lowest setting and heat through for 3–4 minutes, not any longer.

Garnish with lemon wedges and chopped coriander leaves, and eat with naan (see p58).

Lahori fish

In chickpea batter and ajwain seeds

Summer holidays spent with my cousins in Lahore were always a food adventure. This is a city that never stops eating, and one of the most authentic street meals from Lahore's foodie hotspot is this lightly battered chickpea flour fish. The trick to a crispy coating is dipping the fish in rice water (that's the starchy water that's drained off after boiling rice) instead of tap water. An alternative is to mix a teaspoon of cornflour in tap water for a similar effect.

4–6 haddock fillets
juice of ½ lemon
½ tsp ground turmeric
1 tsp salt
100g/3½ oz/generous 1 cup gram flour
2 tbsp rice flour
1 tsp dry-roasted cumin seeds
½ tsp ajwain (carom seeds)
½ tsp red chilli flakes (or more if you like)
100ml/3½ fl oz/scant ½ cup rice water (made by boiling 1 tbsp of rice in 120ml/4 fl oz/½ cup water, straining and reserving the water, or 100ml/3½ fl oz/ scant ½ cup water mixed with 1 tsp cornflour/cornstarch)
50ml/2 fl oz/scant ¼ cup corn oil

Preparation 20 minutes | **Cooking** 10–15 minutes | **Serves** 4–6

Rub the fish with the lemon juice, turmeric and ½ teaspoon salt.

Mix the gram flour, rice flour, cumin, ajwain, red chilli flakes and remaining salt together in a bowl. Pour the rice water into another bowl. Dip the fish into the dry gram flour mix, then in the rice water and repeat again. Continue until all the pieces of fish are covered.

Heat the oil in shallow frying pan over a medium heat and fry the fish for 4–5 minutes on each side until cooked through with a crisp coating. Serve hot with lemon slices.

Kitchen secret

To get a really crisp coating, begin by patting the fish dry with kitchen paper to remove all the non-starchy moisture before dipping into the starch water. If your fish is a little smelly, rub some white vinegar on the fish then rinse under cold running water and pat dry with kitchen paper before coating.

Green masala fish in banana leaves

The Gujarati-speaking Parsi community in Pakistan have a distinct flavour to their cuisine. This is a classic recipe that only seems to vary ever so slightly from one Parsi home to the next. It's a recipe I picked up from friends growing up. You can use a whole fish, or pieces; you can cook the fish on the barbecue, you can shallow-fry, or steam the banana-leaf parcels in a steamer.

4 skinless haddock fillets about
    10–13cm/4–5 inches in length
1 tsp salt
½ tsp ground turmeric
juice of ½ lemon
5 tbsp green chutney (see p146)
4 pieces of fresh banana leaves
3–4 tbsp vegetable oil

Preparation 15 minutes + 1 hour marinating | **Cooking** 10–15 minutes | **Serves** 4

Rub the fish with salt, turmeric and lemon juice. Put the chutney in a large bowl, add the fish and turn to coat. Cover and leave the fish in the chutney to marinate for about 1 hour.

Cut the banana leaves into squares large enough to enclose the fish. Place the fish in the middle of the square, making sure the marinade is covering the fish, then fold and close up using kitchen string or toothpicks.

Heat the oil in a shallow pan with a lid over a medium heat. When hot, reduce the heat to low, add the fish parcels, cover with the lid and cook for about 3–4 minutes. Uncover and cook for a further 4–6 minutes, or until the fish is cooked through.

Serve with plain basmati rice.

Kitchen secret
If you can't find banana leaves then use foil instead. Gently steam the fish parcels in a steamer or bake in a hot oven.

Squid, mussel and prawn biryani

Whenever I make this I'm immediately transported to the silver sands of Seaview Beach in Karachi where I would often devour a picnic of seafood biryani with my hands while enjoying the afternoon sun. The flavours of this biryani are unique due to the green chutney (see p146), which infuses the seafood with freshness and flavour. The addition of lemons with the saffron sets off the herbs in the curry base.

300g/10½ oz/1⅔ cups basmati rice

1 tsp saffron threads

20ml sunflower oil

10 cloves

10 black peppercorns

5cm/2-inch cinnamon stick

5 green cardamom pods

1 tsp cumin seeds

1 tsp coriander (cilantro) seeds

½ tsp ajwain (carom seeds)

2 large red onions, finely chopped

2.5cm/1-inch piece ginger, peeled
and grated

2 garlic, cloves puréed

150g/5½oz green chutney
(see p146)

salt, to taste

200g/7oz/scant 1 cup whole
Greek yogurt

5–6 tbsp water

4 king prawns (shrimp), with shells on

1 squid, cleaned and cut into rings

handful of fresh mussels

2 tbsp rose water or kewra
(screwpine extract)

½ lemon, cut into thin round slices

10 mint leaves

1 tbsp ghee, melted (see p23)

Preparation 20 minutes + 1 hour soaking | **Cooking** 40–45 minutes | **Serves** 6–8

Wash the rice and soak in a bowl of water for 1 hour, then drain, par-boil and drain again. Soak the saffron threads in a bowl of boiled water for 10 minutes.

Heat the oil in a deep saucepan over a medium heat. When hot, add the whole spices and fry for 30 seconds or so until they pop. Add the red onions and cook for 7–10 minutes, or until golden brown.

Reduce the heat to low, add the ginger and garlic and stir-fry for about 20 seconds, or until the raw smell disappears and the garlic and ginger start to brown. If they are burning add a couple of splashes of water.

Mix the green chutney, salt and yogurt together in a bowl. Add to the pan with the red onion mixture, then stir and cook over a low heat, stirring occasionally, for 15–20 minutes, or until the oil rises to the top. If the curry is too dry, add the water and stir. Keep simmering over a low heat until the curry is a medium green colour with oil floating on the surface. Turn the heat off. The curry should be a thick consistency. If it is not, continue to cook for a few minutes without a lid.

Put the prawns, squid and mussels on top of the curry. Spoon the drained rice evenly over the seafood and curry, then pour the saffron and rose water around the top of the rice. Arrange the lemons and mint leaves here and there into the rice.

Pour the melted ghee over, cover the pan with a large piece of foil firmly around the edges, then tightly cover with the lid. Turn the heat to very low and cook in its own steam for 8–10 minutes. Turn off the heat and, using a fork, gently mix the rice with the seafood and curry. Serve hot with raita.

Fish kofta curry

These koftas can be eaten on their own, or added to this lightly spiced tomato sauce and served with rice. They're beautiful when made using any white fish, but they can also be made with salmon if you prefer.

For the koftas

150g/5½oz white fish (haddock or cod) fillets, steamed and flaked with a fork
2 tbsp breadcrumbs
3 tbsp cooked, mashed potato
1 tsp dry-roasted cumin seeds
½ tsp ajwain (carom seeds)
1 tsp salt, or to taste
2 tbsp chopped coriander (cilantro) leaves
6 mint leaves, finely chopped
½ green chilli, finely chopped
1 tbsp tamarind paste (or homemade pulp, see p23)
3 tbsp semolina
1 egg, whipped
5 tbsp vegetable oil, for frying

For the curry

4 tbsp coconut oil or vegetable oil
1 tsp coriander (cilantro) seeds
1 tsp mustard seeds
1 tsp nigella seeds
7–8 fresh curry leaves
1 red onion, finely chopped
½ tsp each of grated ginger and crushed garlic
3–4 tomatoes, finely chopped
1 tbsp tomato purée
½ tsp salt, or to taste
½ tsp red chilli powder
½ tsp ground turmeric

To garnish

handful of fresh tender coriander (cilantro) leaves with stems, chopped
4–5 mint leaves, chopped

Preparation 25 minutes | **Cooking** 35–40 minutes | **Serves** 6

To make the koftas, combine all the ingredients, except the semolina, in a bowl by hand, squeezing the ingredients together so they hold.

Spread the semolina out on a plate. Take about 1 tablespoon of the fish mixture and, using your hand, roll into golf ball-sized ball, then roll in the semolina and place on a plate. Continue until all the fish mixture has been used up.

Heat the oil in a frying pan over a medium heat. When hot, reduce the heat, add a few fish balls at a time and cook for 3–5 minutes until golden brown. Remove from the pan with a slotted spoon and drain on kitchen paper.

To make the curry, heat the oil in a saucepan with a lid over a medium heat. When hot, add the spices and cook for 30 seconds or so until they pop. Add the onion and cook for 7–10 minutes until light brown. Add the ginger and garlic and fry for a few seconds until light brown.

Add the tomatoes and tomato purée, salt, red chilli and turmeric and cook, stirring, and adding a few splashes of water if the juice from the tomatoes runs dry. Continue to stir-fry until the oil rises to the top and you're left with a thick sauce, about 3–5 minutes.

Once this sauce is cooked, pop in the fish balls and, using a spoon, gently coat in the sauce. Reduce the heat to very low, cover the pan with the lid and simmer for 3–4 minutes, or until the fish balls are heated through.

Garnish with chopped coriander leaves and mint and serve with rice.

Sindhi barbecued fish

Tossed in rice flour

This recipe is inspired by a dish from the Sindh province using palla (a type of fish rarely found outside South Asia), which is coated with a delicious crusty blend of spice. You can use fillets of white fish such as plaice, haddock or coley. And you can also try using the spice mix on a whole fish before baking or frying.

1 tbsp coriander (cilantro) seeds
2 tsp fennel seeds
1 bay leaf
½ tsp cumin seeds
1cm/½-inch cinnamon stick
1 tsp salt
2 garlic cloves
2 red chillies, deseeded
1 tsp ground turmeric
1 tsp chilli powder
juice of 1 lime
2 tbsp rice flour
2 tbsp water
4 large white fish fillets such as plaice or haddock
50ml/2 fl oz/scant ¼ cup vegetable oil, for drying

Preparation 10–12 minutes | **Cooking** 10–15 minutes | **Serves** 4

Grind the coriander seeds, fennel seeds, bay leaf, cumin seeds and cinnamon together in a spice grinder until finely ground. Add about 2 teaspoons of this spice blend to a mortar and pestle with the salt, garlic, red chillies, turmeric and chilli powder and grind into a fine paste while adding lime juice to moisten. Add the rice flour and the water and mix together into a thick paste. Put the paste into a large shallow bowl, then add the fish and turn until the fish is coated all over with the paste.

Heat the oil in a frying pan over a medium heat. When hot, reduce the heat slightly to medium low, add the spiced fish and fry for 4–5 minutes on each side. You should have a thick crispy crust on each side. Carefully remove the fish from the pan and drain on kitchen paper before serving.

Fish tikkas

With turmeric and Kashmiri chilli

Ajwain (carom) seeds and fish are a perfect match. and these tikkas should be made using a firm white fish such as cod and cooked on the barbecue or under the grill.

juice of 1 lemon
½ tsp red chilli flakes
1 tsp dry-roasted coriander
   (cilantro) seeds
1 tsp Kashmiri chilli powder
¼ tsp ground turmeric
¾ tsp ajwain (carom seeds)
½ tsp dry-roasted cumin seeds
½ tsp garlic purée
½ tsp ginger paste
2 tbsp whole Greek yogurt
1 tbsp chopped mint
150g/5½oz firm flesh white
   fish cubes
3 tbsp mustard oil or vegetable oil

Preparation 10 minutes + 30 minutes marinating | **Cooking** 15 minutes | **Serves** 4–6

Make the marinade by combining all the ingredients except the fish and oil together in a large bowl. Add the fish, turn to coat, cover and allow to marinate in the fridge for about 30 minutes.

Light a barbecue or indoor grill. Brush the fish with mustard or vegetable oil, and grill for 3–5 minutes on either side until it is caramelised and light brown around the edges.

Serve with red onion, green chilli and radishes and a squeeze of lime, if you like.

Lemon pickle fish

1 pickled lemon (see p150) or ½
   lemon boiled in water until skin is
   soft (about 1 hour)
1 tsp salt
½ tsp Kashmiri red chilli powder
1 tbsp mustard oil
½ tsp dry-roasted cumin seeds
½ tsp dry-roasted coriander seeds
4 halibut, sole or sea bass fillets
   (without skin)
50ml/2 fl oz/scant ¼ cup vegetable
   oil (if frying fish)

Preparation 10 minutes (if using pre-made pickle) | **Cooking** 10–15 minutes | **Serves** 4

If you want to grill the fish, rather than griddle or fry it, preheat the grill to high.

Pound the pickled lemon, if using, in a mortar and pestle until soft and pulpy. If using boiled lemon, cut the peel into tiny pieces. Add all the remaining ingredients except the fish and oil, mix together and smear over the fish to coat.

Depending on your cooking method of choice, add the oil and then heat the griddle pan or frying pan. Grill, griddle or fry the fish for 10 minutes, or until light golden and crisp around the edges.

Mummy's whole fish

With spiced red onion and tomato topping

A whole fish (or fish steaks) topped with spiced tomato and red onion is a quick and delicious way to add Pakistani flavour to seafood – this one is a staple in my mother's home. You can use red snapper, mackerel or rainbow trout (whole or in fillets), or halibut or hake works just as well.

1 whole gutted red snapper (or fish of your choice)
juice of 1 lemon
1 tsp sea salt
1 tsp red chilli powder
1 tsp ground turmeric
5–6 tbsp vegetable oil
1½ tsp cumin seeds
2 garlic cloves, thinly sliced
3 red onions, cut into rings
½ tsp ajwain seed
5 large tomatoes on the vine, chopped
1 tbsp tomato purée

To garnish
½ bunch of coriander (cilantro) leaves, roughly chopped
2 green chillies, finely chopped
2.5cm/1-inch piece ginger, peeled and cut into julienne
juice of ½ lemon

Preparation 15–20 minutes | **Cooking** 20 minutes fillet, 50 minutes whole fish | **Serves** 3–4

Rub the fish with lemon juice, salt, chilli powder and turmeric. Place on a plate, cover loosely and set aside until ready to cook.

Preheat the oven to 180°C/350°F/gas mark 4.

Heat the oil in a frying pan over a medium heat. When hot, add the cumin seeds and allow to splutter for 30 seconds. Add the garlic and cook for a few seconds; do not allow to burn. Add the onions and cook for 10 minutes, or until slightly caramelised.

Add the ajwain seeds and chopped tomatoes and cook for 5–6 minutes, or until the tomatoes are soft and the oil rises to the top. Add the tomato purée and cook for a further 3–4 minutes until everything is red and bubbly. Turn off the heat.

Top the fish with this tomato mixture, then place the fish in a large baking dish, cover with foil and cook in the hot oven for 45 minutes if the fish is whole, 15–20 minutes if the fish is in pieces. Check to see if the fish is cooked through. For the last 4–5 minutes remove the foil and allow the topping to caramelise.

Garnish with chopped coriander, green chilli, ginger julienne and a squeeze of lemon and serve hot.

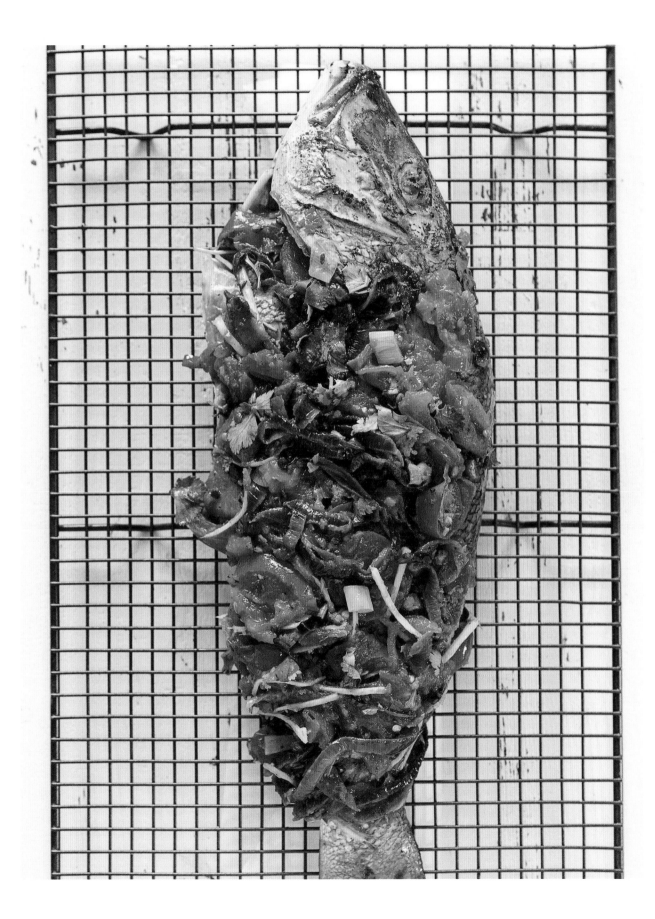

My grandmother's garden
Vegetables, fruit and salad

Endless summers were spent strolling through what seemed like vast fields filled with hand-sown vegetable patches, innumerable fruit-laden trees and lovingly tended flowers. This was my world of seasonal natural wonders, which Nani (my maternal grandmother) cherished and devoted much of her time to.

The warmer months saw trees heavy with luscious indigenous Sindhri mangos, caramel-flavoured chickoos (a tropical fruit also known as sapodilla), sweet and sour falsa berries and mouth-drying jamuns (sweet, tangy local berries). This sun-drenched feast was followed by sharifa (custard apples), guavas and pomegranate in the cooler months.

Alongside the bounty from the trees and bushes flourished Nani's own vegetables. Potatoes, beans, carrots… there was always something being sown into or tugged out of the earth. It was a sensory experience to walk through her garden: I would revel in the scent of curry leaves and feel soothed by the aroma of the tiny lemons peeking through intensely green leaves, while my favourite, the invitingly succulent karela (gourd), would beg to be picked and taken to the kitchen.

Perhaps the real beauty of a Pakistani garden is the scent of blossoms – large clusters of red, orange and pink bougainvillea, violet and oxblood pansies, and the rich, purplish-red desi gulab. But in Nani's garden the most memorable flower was the motia – it's from the jasmine family but much fuller in both appearance and aroma. Its tight buds came alive at nightfall and filled the sunset air with its heady essence. At dusk she would pick them and arrange them in a terracotta bowl of water, their beauty slowly growing through the evening, enveloping her bedroom with an exotic fragrance.

Memories of the garden, its flavours, its beauty and its scents inspire the recipes in this chapter.

Kalay chanay

Black chickpea with white poppy seeds and red onion

The nutty skin of black chickpea, the bite of poppy seeds, the sharpness of tamarind: kalay chanay is a surprising sensation. My mother cooks this during Ramazan (the period of fasting for Muslims): it's a snack to bless the table, and with its 'garam' qualities it brings heat to the soul.

Preparation 45 minutes + overnight soaking | **Cooking** 25 minutes | **Serves** 4–5

500g/1¼lb/2⅔ cups dried black chickpeas (available in most South Asian stores)
2 tbsp vegetable oil
1 tsp cumin seeds
½ tsp nigella seeds (kalongi)
2 tbsp white poppy seeds (available in most South Asian stores)
1–2 red onions, cut into fine rings
100g/3½oz garlic, tamarind and red chilli chutney (see p150)

To garnish
chopped coriander (cilantro) leaves
chopped green chillies
2 medium tomatoes, deseeded and chopped into medium pieces

Soak the black chickpeas overnight in a bowl of water. The next day, drain, put in a large saucepan, pour in 500ml/17 fl oz/2 cups water, or enough to cover them and bring to the boil. Cook for 30–40 minutes, or until soft. These don't get as soft as regular chickpeas and retain a slight bite. Drainn and set aside.

Heat the oil in a saucepan over a medium heat. When hot, add the cumin, nigella and poppy seeds and fry for about 1 minute until they pop. Add half the red onions and cook, stirring constantly, for 3 minutes, or until just soft. Allow them to retain a little crunch. Add the boiled black chickpeas, the remaining red onions, and stir through until hot.

Turn off the heat and add the tamarind chutney (see p150) and garnishes. Serve warm or cold.

Fruit chaat

Spicy fruit salad with masala dressing

Seasonal fruit in piquant spices, citrus juice and salt is a personal childhood treat. Rather like Marmite, you will either love it or hate it. You can add boiled chickpeas or potatoes, but personally I prefer just the fruit version. A true South Asian classic.

Preparation 15–30 minutes | **Serves** 3–4

1 mango, cut into small chunks
1 banana, sliced
1 guava, cut into small chunks
1 small orange, deseeded and cut into small chunks
1 apple, cut into chunks
10–15 grapes, cut into half
juice of ½ lemon
juice of ½ lime
juice of ½ orange
1½ tsp chaat masala (see p26)
½ tsp caster (superfine) sugar
½ tsp dry-roasted cumin seeds
6–7 mint leaves, finely chopped
2 tbsp pomegranate seeds

Place all the fruit in a bowl with the chickpeas and/or boiled potatoes, if using.

Squeeze the citrus juices over the fruit and season with the chaat masala, sugar and dry-roasted cumin. Mix well and chill in the fridge for about 30 minutes before serving to allow the juices to mix well with the fruit.

To serve, sprinkle over the chopped mint leaves and pomegranate seeds and serve cold.

Kitchen secret
You can make this an hour before you want to serve it to give the fruit a chance to soak up the juice and become infused with flavour.

Dadi's turnip kebabs

These kebabs are a labour of love. Make them when you have a spare afternoon, as the process is time consuming – but don't be put off, they are worth it. My Dadi (paternal grandmother) made these often, seemingly effortlessly, and my mother loosely wrote down her recipe years ago, which I've used here. She still has that cherished scrap of paper today, and still makes them fondly.

50g/1¾oz/¼ cup chana daal
2 dried red chillies
100ml/3½ fl oz/½ cup water, plus
    extra 60ml/2¼ fl oz/¼ cup
    (optional)
3 medium top-shaped turnips,
    peeled and cut into quarters
1 Maris Piper potato, peeled, boiled
    and mashed
1 tbsp ground anardana (dried
    pomegranate)
1 tsp each of dry-roasted and roughly
    ground cumin and coriander
    (cilantro) seeds
¾ tsp garam masala
salt, to taste
1 tbsp ground anardana (dried
    pomegranate) or juice of ½ lemon
2–3 spring onions (scallions), finely
    chopped with greens
1 green chilli, finely chopped
handful of coriander (cilantro) leaves,
    finely chopped
10 mint leaves, finely chopped
50ml/2 fl oz/scant ¼ cup vegetable
    oil, for frying
3 tbsp cornflour (cornstarch)
1 egg, beaten (optional)

Preparation 1 hour + overnight soaking | **Cooking** 30 minutes | **Serves** 8–10

Soak the chana daal overnight in a bowl of water. The next day, drain and boil with the dried red chillies for 15 minutes, or until dry and cooked. Drain and set aside.

Pour the measured water into a saucepan with a lid, add the cut turnip, cover and cook over a medium heat until all the water has evaporated. If the turnip is still raw add the extra water and cook until the water has evaporated and the turnip is cooked. This should take about 20–25 minutes. Mash the turnip, then place in a muslin cloth and squeeze out any excess liquid until it is completely dry. Place in a bowl, add the mashed potato and cooked chana daal together with the remaining ingredients, except the oil, cornflour or egg. Mix and knead until everything is combined.

Mould about 2 tablespoons of the mixture into a round ball then flatten into a burger patty shape. Place on a plate and repeat until all the mixture is used up. These can now be frozen or cooked straight away. Heat the oil in a frying pan. Spread the cornflour or egg out on a plate. Dip each kebab into the cornflour or egg, lightly coating each side then place into the hot frying pan and cook for 3–4 minutes on each side, or until medium brown. Eat warm with lemon wedges, chutney, daal and rice or any choice of bread.

Kitchen secret

These freeze really well. Freeze before frying, and allow to partially defrost when you are ready to use them. Then coat with egg or cornflour and fry gently – do not overhandle them. The key is to ensure that all the moisture is squeezed out when you are preparing them, so that they hold together when frying.

Stuffed karela
Bitter gourd filled with spiced chana daal

The rather scaly karela is an acquired taste. It's unpleasantly bitter if not prepared well, but if cooked correctly it's a vegetable with an ability to absorb any flavour without losing its voice. You can also try this recipe with hollowed courgette or pepper if karela doesn't appeal, and the daal can also be replaced with pre-cooked keema (p80).

For the bitter gourd
4 bitter gourd
4 tbsp salt

For the chana daal filling
100g/3½ oz/scant ½ cup chana daal
100ml/3½ fl oz/scant ½ cup vegetable oil or 2 tbsp coconut oil
1 tsp nigella seeds
1 tsp cumin seeds
1 tsp aniseed
½ tsp fenugreek seeds
3 large red onions, cut into thin slices
1 tsp grated ginger
1 tsp crushed garlic
3 tomatoes, roughly chopped
1 tsp dhania mirchi blend (see p27)

To garnish
1 tbsp chopped green chillies
1 tbsp chopped fresh tender coriander (cilantro) with stems

Preparation 50 minutes + overnight soaking | **Cooking** 45 minutes | **Serves** 4

Soak the chana daal overnight in a bowl of water. The next day, drain and set aside.

To remove the bitter taste from the gourd, cut it lengthways, scoop out the seeds, sprinkle with the salt on each half and leave in a colander for about 30 minutes. Wash and set aside.

To prepare the daal filling, heat a frying pan over a medium heat and add half the oil. When hot, add the nigella seeds, cumin, aniseed and fenugreek seeds and fry for 30 seconds. Add the onion, ginger and garlic and stir-fry for 8–10 minutes until the onions are soft and the raw smell of ginger and garlic disappears. Add the drained chana daal, stir for 3–5 minutes, then add the tomatoes and the dhania mirchi blend and cook for a further 7–8 minutes, or until the tomatoes are soft and all moisture has evaporated. The daal should now be cooked through and not mushy.

Using a teaspoon, fill one bitter gourd at a time with the filling, making sure that all the filling reaches the corners. Using the string, tie up the bitter gourd gently to help keep the daal inside while cooking.

To cook, heat a large frying pan with a lid with oil over a low-medium heat. When hot, add all the bitter gourds and cook gently, partially covered with the lid, until the skin is dark brown and crisp.

Cut the string, garnish with chopped chillies and coriander and serve hot with rice or naan (see p58).

Crispy bhindi
Chickpea batter okra

A moreish fried okra recipe: you just can't make enough! It's wonderful with a simple daal and basmati rice for a light lunch. A recipe inspired by visits to my best friend Shazia's house, where her mother, Samina Khala, often made this for us.

250g/9oz gram flour

50g/1¾oz rice flour or cornflour (cornstarch), optional

1 tsp red chilli powder

½ tsp ground turmeric

1 tsp salt

1 tsp dry-roasted cumin seeds

50ml/2 fl oz/scant ¼ cup water

50g/1¾oz okra, washed and dried completely before cutting, top, tailed and cut lengthways into 4 thin strips

250ml/9 fl oz/1 cup vegetable oil, for frying

To garnish

1 tsp chaat masala (see p26)

½ lemon

Preparation 15 minutes | **Cooking** 15 minutes | **Serves** 6

Mix all the dry ingredients (except the okra) together in a large bowl and add the measured water or enough to make a very thick batter.

Dip all the okra into the batter and turn until it is coated. Heat the oil in a frying pan over a medium heat. When hot, add the okra a piece at a time into the oil and cook until light golden brown. Remove with a slotted spoon and drain on kitchen paper.

Serve hot with a sprinkling of chaat masala and a gentle squeeze of lemon juice.

Mooli and tarbuz salad

White radish, watermelon and black salt

I was once invited to stay with Lahori philanthropist and socialite Yousaf Salahuddin, and experienced his breathtaking 'haveli' (historical mansion) and open-hearted hospitality. He served a simple combination of white mooli and black salt, and the memory inspires this unusual salad.

Preparation 15 minutes | **Serves** 4–6

½ watermelon, cut into medium chunks
1 mooli (daikon), peeled and cut into thin slices
Juice of ½ lime
½ tsp freshly ground black peppercorns
1 tsp kalanamak (black salt) or sea salt
mint leaves, to garnish

Make sure that the watermelon and mooli are chilled before preparing. Chop the watermelon, slice the mooli and place into a bowl.

Add the lime juice and toss. Add the ground peppercorns and kalanamak and toss together. Serve garnished with mint leaves.

Sarson ka saag

Mustard leaf stir-fry

This is a Punjabi village staple made with mustard greens from the boundless fields of that fertile land. Its flavour comes from seasonal ingredients and traditional cooking methods. It's a mix of mustard greens, spinach and corn greens, but can be made with just spinach and fenugreek.

Preparation 15 minutes | **Cooking** 15 minutes | **Serves** 3–4

700g/1½ lb mustard greens or spinach
200g/7oz spinach (omit if using spinach instead of mustard greens)
200g/7oz fresh fenugreek leaves (if using dried try only use 100g/3½oz)
2 green chillies
½ tsp ground turmeric
½ tsp red chilli powder
salt, to taste
50g/2oz cornmeal/polenta
2 tbsp ghee (see p23)
1 tsp cumin seeds
1 tsp coriander seeds
½ tsp mustard seeds
1 medium red onion, finely chopped
1 tsp each of grated ginger and crushed garlic
1 tbsp homemade butter (or unsalted butter)
½ tsp garam masala
1cm/½-inch piece of ginger, peeled and cut into julienne

Steam the spinach, mustard greens and fenugreek, if using, in a steamer for 7–10 minutes, or until soft and wilted. Allow to cool, then squeeze out all the moisture from the greens until quite dry over a bowl and set this water aside.

Place the spinach, greens, green chillies, turmeric and red chilli powder in a saucepan with 50ml/2 fl oz/scant ¼ cup of the reserved water. Add the salt and bring to the boil. Cook until all the water has evaporated then blitz in a blender to a purée. Add the cornmeal and stir to combine.

Heat the ghee in a frying pan over a medium heat. When hot, add the cumin, coriander and mustard seeds and allow them to splutter for 30 seconds. Add the onion, ginger and garlic and stir-fry for 7 minutes until the onions are softened. Add the greens purée and stir and cook until the purée is warmed through.

Serve topped with a knob of butter, sprinkled with garam masala and ginger julienne. This is eaten with the makkai ki roti on p59.

Crispy chapati kachumber salad

This popular South Asian salad is made from uniformly diced pieces of fresh vegetables, lots of lemon and dry-roasted cumin. It's a great accompaniment to barbecue dishes and biryanis. Inspired by Italian panzanella, I've added crispy leftover chapati (or use paratha) for texture.

Preparation 20 minutes | **Serves** 4–6

2 large tomatoes, deseeded and finely chopped
1 large red onion, finely chopped
1 cucumber, deseeded and finely chopped
1–2 thin green chillies, deseeded and finely chopped
2 tbsp fresh pomegranate seeds
juice of 1 lemon, plus wedges, to garnish
salt, to taste
1 tsp dry-roasted cumin seeds, roughly ground
½ tsp chaat masala (see p26)
1 chapati bread, toasted and broken into small 2.5cm/1-inch pieces

Combine the first five ingredients with the lemon juice, cumin, salt and chaat masala. Chill until serving. Add the broken chapati pieces before serving and stir well. Garnish with lemon wedges.

Radish, red onion and green chilli salad

This is not really a dressed-up salad, but more a pretty plate of Pakistani salad essentials (which would almost always be homegrown in my parents' garden). The simplicity and freshness of the ingredients complements all Pakistani dishes. Use them fresh, cut them rustically.

Preparation 10 minutes | **Serves** 4

10 radishes, finely sliced
1 red onion, finely sliced
2 green chillies, finely chopped
½ lemon
½ tsp dry-roasted cumin seeds
salt, to taste

Assemble the salad in a serving bowl and top with lemon juice, cumin and salt.

This goes very well alongside beef meatball pulao (see p70), railway mutton curry (see p79), Punjabi aloo gosht (see p83), chicken salan (see p104), Sindhi mutton biryani (see p160) and beef kofta curry (see p175).

Aloo bharta

Mashed potato with cumin and crushed chilli

I call this a spiced Pakistani mashed potato. My grandmother would make it with leftover mash – or make it fresh on a rainy day when I craved spice. I also make an avocado version (see Kitchen secret below), which works as a dip with crisped pitta or as a side dish. You can use this mash to recreate a street snack sold on roadsides called aloo bonda: just make round balls from the mash, dip in pakora batter (p44) and deep-fry. Served with green chutney (p146), it's always a treat.

3 Maris Piper potatoes, peeled and
    cut into 4 pieces
1 tbsp coconut oil
1 tsp cumin seeds
1 small garlic clove, chopped
1 small red onion, finely chopped
¼ tsp ground turmeric
5 curry leaves
salt, to taste
1 tsp crushed dried red chilli
2 tbsp finely chopped
    coriander (cilantro) leaves
1 tsp finely chopped ginger
10 mint leaves, finely chopped
1 spring onion (scallion), finely
    chopped
1 tsp dry-roasted cumin seeds,
    roughly ground in mortar
    and pestle
2 green chillies, deseeded and
    finely chopped
1 tsp amchoor (dried mango powder)
    (or the juice of ½ lime)
1 tsp dry-roasted coriander seeds,
    ground

Preparation 15 minutes | **Cooking** 20 minutes | **Serves** 4–6

Boil the potatoes in a large saucepan until soft, then drain, return to the pan and mash them well, cover and set aside.

Heat a shallow pan with the coconut oil over a medium heat. When hot, add the cumin seeds and allow to splutter for 30 seconds. Add the garlic and onion and cook for 7–9 minutes until soft and light brown around the edges.

Add the turmeric and stir the onions, then add the curry leaves and allow to splutter. Remove the pan from the heat.

Heat the mashed potato in a pan or microwave until piping hot.

Stir the onion mixture into the mashed potato until combined. Season with salt and add the remaining ingredients. Serve warm.

Kitchen secret

To make an avocado version, add mustard seeds to the oil at the start, allow to splutter, then add the remaining ingredients. Omit the amchoor and mint leaves.

Sindhi karri

Yogurt and turmeric soup with curry leaves and egg

Known as karri in Sindh, this is a lovely combination of whipped natural yogurt with turmeric, tempered with infused oil (it may sound odd, but using yogurt that is a few days old works very well here). Traditionally, chickpea dumplings and seasonal vegetables are included too, and some families add boiled eggs. My mother would occasionally add boiled eggs, which were lightly fried, cut in half and dropped into the karri. This is a simple dish, best served with plain basmati rice.

340g/14oz/1¾ cups whole plain yogurt

1 litre/1¾ pints/4 cups cool water

salt, to taste

½ tsp red chilli powder

1 heaped tsp ground turmeric

½ heaped tsp each of grated ginger and garlic purée

1 tbsp semolina

1 tbsp chickpea flour

50ml/2 fl oz/scant ¼ cup sunflower oil

½ tsp fenugreek seeds

50g/1¾ oz/scant ½ cup peas

100g/3½ oz carrot batons (sticks)

1 Maris Piper potato, peeled and cut into batons (sticks)

3 hard-boiled eggs which have been fried in oil and browned separately

1 tbsp chopped coriander (cilantro) leaves, to garnish

For the bhagar (tempering)

50ml/2 fl oz/scant ¼ cup sunflower oil

1 garlic clove, thinly sliced

1 tsp mustard seeds

1 tsp cumin seeds

4 long dried red chillies

5–6 fresh curry leaves

Preparation 20 minutes | **Cooking** 30 minutes | **Serves** 6–8

Put the yogurt into a large bowl with the cool water and whisk until combined. This creates a thin 'lassi'. Add salt to taste, then add the red chilli powder, turmeric, ginger, garlic, semolina and chickpea flour and whisk until combined. Strain this mixture through a sieve to remove any lumps.

Heat the sunflower oil in a saucepan with a lid over a medium heat. When hot, add a few fenugreek seeds and allow to splutter. Take them out with a slotted spoon once the oil is fragrant, leaving them in will make the dish bitter.

Pour the strained yellow yogurt into the oil and cook over a very low heat, stirring occasionally. Increase the heat slightly to medium low and cook gently for 25–30 minutes, or until the karri is thick and fragrant. Meanwhile, par-boil the vegetables and prepare the eggs.

Once the vegetables are cooked, about 10 minutes, the karri is ready to bhagar (temper). Add the eggs to the karri before tempering.

To temper, heat the remaining oil in a small frying pan over a medium heat . When hot, add the garlic and fry for 30 seconds, or until light brown. Add the mustard seeds, cumin and dried red chilli and lastly the curry leaves. Quickly pour this on top of the karri, then cover the pan with the lid for a few minutes. Garnish with coriander leaves and enjoy as a soup or with rice.

Moong daal

310g/3½ oz/scant ½ cup moong
    daal (without husk)
2 garlic cloves, thinly sliced
½ tsp ground turmeric
salt, to taste
2 tsp ghee or vegetable oil mixed
    with 1 tsp butter (see p23)
1 tsp cumin seeds
2–3 dried red chillies
3–4 curry leaves, fresh (optional)
1 tbsp chopped coriander (cilantro)
1 green chilli, chopped
½ tsp garam masala (see p26)
handful of fried crispy red onions

Preparation 10 minutes | **Cooking** 25 minutes | **Serves** 3–4

Put the daal into a saucepan and pour in enough water to cover. Add 1 sliced garlic clove and the turmeric and mix well. Bring the daal to the boil and cook over a medium heat for 12–15 minutes, stirring occasionally, until the daal is cooked through. Using the back of a spoon, mash the daal then pour into a serving dish and add salt to taste.

Heat the ghee and oil and butter in a small frying pan or tarka pan over a medium heat. When hot, add the cumin and allow to splutter for 30 seconds. Add the rest of the garlic and brown slightly, then add the red chillies for a few seconds, and lastly the curry leaves for just a second. Pour over the daal immediately. Garnish with chopped coriander, chilli, garam masala and crispy fried onions. Eat hot with bread or rice as an accompaniment or by itself.

Dry cooked maash daal
Tempering of cumin, coriander and ginger

340g/14oz/1¾ cups maash or
    urid daal
salt, to taste
½ tsp red chilli powder
1 tsp each of ground cumin and
    coriander seeds
½ tsp ground turmeric
2 tbsp ghee (see p23)
1½ tsp cumin seeds
2 large garlic cloves, thinly sliced
2–4 dried red chillies
1 tsp garam masala
½ bunch of coriander (cilantro)
    leaves, chopped
2.5-cm/1-inch piece ginger, peeled
and finely cut into slivers
juice of ½ lime

Preparation 10 minutes + 30 minutes soaking | **Cooking** 25 minutes | **Serves** 3–4

Soak the daal in a bowl of water for 30 minutes, then drain. Put the daal in a large saucepan with the salt, chilli powder, cumin, coriander, turmeric and 500ml/17 fl oz/2 cups boiling water, or enough to just cover the daal. Cook over a medium heat for about 15 minutes, or until soft, cooked through and all the water has been absorbed. Pour into a serving bowl and add more salt, if necessary.

For the bhagar (tempering), heat the ghee in a small frying pan over a medium heat. When hot, add the cumin seeds and allow to splutter for 30 seconds. Add the garlic and fry until light brown. Add the dried chillies – don't let these burn – and fry for 5 seconds. Pour immediately over the daal and stir. Garnish with a sprinkle of garam masala, chopped coriander leaves, ginger slivers and lime juice.

Homegrown guavas
Chutney and pickles

Pickling is the art of preserving the seasons. Pakistani 'achars' (pickles) are creations that begin upon a canvas of seasonal produce; they're then splashed with spice and layered over with sweet and savoury ingredients. The result is a balance of piquancy and flavour that means Pakistani pickles aren't relegated to an accompaniment, but are sophisticated enough to serve as a humble meal atop a piece of roti or rice.

In restaurants in the West we're served up a crispy mountain of poppadoms, mango pickle and chutney for starters, but in Pakistan this would be unheard of: instead preserves are presented as delicate morsels at the side of a piled dinner plate, adding extra enticement with their aroma as well as further layers of taste. In my family, food was served with a marinated pickle of homegrown raw mango, guava or beetroot, or a fresh chutney of seasonal berries like falsa or amla, fresh coriander, mint or tamarind, and dates. The preparation of these was almost ritualistic.

In summer, chutneys were artfully pureed by hand on our family heirloom 'sil batta', a big stone block and cylinder used like a mortar and pestle. In spring fruit was brought straight from the trees, made into pickles by all the women in the family and distributed to good friends and neighbours to be enjoyed through the year. And of all the wonders in my Nani's (maternal grandmother) garden, it's the tiny Pakistani lemons that were most revered – in fact, soon after she passed, the tree wilted away within a matter of weeks. I still make the pickle she made with these precious lemons, and that way the bittersweet memories remain.

Few meals were ever served without the distinctive flavour of preserved fruit and vegetables, and the authenticity of the recipes in this chapter are faithful to the memory of family meals growing up in Pakistan.

Green chutney

Coriander, coconut and chilli

This is a classic green chutney, aromatic and exotic, and with many uses. You can make it as dip, side sauce or marinade, or with fish dishes (see p109) – if you want a lighter, less spiced option, just mix with 2–3 tablespoons of plain yogurt.

I large bunch of coriander (cilantro) leaves
10–12 mint leaves
I small green chilli, deseeded (optional)
½ tbsp brown sugar or jaggery
½ tsp ground turmeric
I tsp dry-roasted cumin seeds
I tsp salt
2 tbsp unsweetened desiccated (dry) coconut
juice of ½ lime
4 tbsp water

Preparation 5–7 minutes | **Makes about** 150–200ml/5–7 fl oz/⅔–scant I cup

Blitz all the ingredients in a blender until it is smooth. This is best used immediately but can be stored in an airtight container in the fridge for up to 4–5 days.

Fermented mustard seed and carrot relish

This salad can be eaten fresh, or left to ferment for 10 to 15 days. The fermentation happens through the yellow mustard seeds and turmeric. The flavour is pungent to begin with, but mellows as days go by.

3 carrots, cut into matchsticks
I tbsp yellow mustard seeds, crushed roughly in a mortar and pestle
juice of ½ lemon
I tsp sea salt
I heaped tsp ground turmeric
I garlic clove, roughly chopped
½ tsp crushed red chilli flakes

Preparation 15 minutes + 2 days fermenting | **Serves** 4–5

Put all the ingredients into a large, non-metallic bowl and toss until everything is mixed well. Either eat immediately or cover with clingfilm or with another ceramic plate and set aside in a cool place to ferment for up to 2 days. Toss the mixture every day.

This keeps for up to a month in a cool, dry place or in the fridge. Keep in a bowl covered with another plate, or cling film, but not foil as it reacts with the pickle.

Carrot murraba

With sugar, lime and saffron

This is a sweet pickle, and is quite different from most other chutneys as the carrots are cooked in sugar syrup that is infused with saffron. Carrot murraba pairs well with spicy curries, biryani and vegetable side dishes.

Preparation 20–25 minutes | **Preservation** Consume within a week | **Serves** 3–4

100g/3½oz/½ cup caster (superfine) sugar
about 25ml/1 fl oz/2 tbsp water
1 large pinch of saffron threads
3 carrots, cut into thin julliene or grated medium
juice of ½ lime

Put the sugar into a saucepan over a low heat and add enough water (about 25ml/1 fl oz/2 tablespoons) to soak the sugar, but not cover it. Stir until the sugar has dissolved.

Add the saffron, stir, and add the carrots and cook for 3–4 minutes. Add the lime and stir.

Pour the mixture into a clean sterilised bottle or jar and store in the fridge for up to a week.

Green chilli and beetroot pickle

This uses a simple South Asian oil-based pickling technique. It's a pickle both my grandmothers made, both using seasonal homegrown beetroot… but never homegrown chilli, as my Dadi (paternal grandmother) always said: never grow chilli at home, it causes couples to fight!

Preparation 20 minutes | **Preservation** 2 weeks–consume within 6 months | **Serves** 3–4

2–3 tbsp mustard oil
½ tsp mustard seeds
½ cumin seeds
½ nigella seeds
½ aniseed
½ tsp coriander (cilantro) seeds
2–3 fresh beetroot, peeled and cut into tiny squares
4 green chillies
salt, to taste
½ tsp ground turmeric

Heat the oil in a frying pan over a medium heat. When hot, add all the seeds and fry for 30 seconds until they pop. Add the beetroot, chillies, salt and turmeric and warm through.

Spoon the pickle into a sterilised jar and keep in a cool place for up to 6 months.

Nani's salted lemon preserve

Regular lemons can be used for this gorgeous pickle, but lime-sized Pakistani lemons are available in some South Asian stores and they pack a real punch. The intensity of this preserve is both wonderful as a pickle, or you can use in a curry or a tagine-style dish, or a fish dish (see p121).

12 small South Asian lemons or
6 lemons
4 tbsp sea salt
10 green chillies

Preparation 10–15 minutes + 2 weeks standing | **Serves** 4–10

If using South Asian lemons, combine them with salt in a bowl, then add the chillies. If using regular lemons, cut the lemons into quarters then add the salt and chillies. Toss well and transfer to a large sterilised preserving jar. Shake the jar every day and move the lemons around. They will release liquid, which is normal.

After 2 weeks the lemons should be sufficiently pickled; however, the longer you leave them the more intensely pickled they'll become. Don't use a metallic utensil to remove the lemons from the jar as it reacts with the pickle, and ensure that the jar is tightly sealed after using. Store for up to a year.

Lasan ki chutney
Garlic, tamarind and red chilli

This chutney goes well with something simple like a pulao or daal. Boiling dried chilli rather than using fresh chilli makes for a more intense chutney. In Pakistan we use round dried red chillies (but any dried red chillies work) and freshly pulped tamarind instead of store-bought pastes.

4 tbsp tamarind pulp (from ½
block dried tamarind, see p23)
250ml/9 fl oz/1 cup hot water
10–14 round dried red chillies or
any dried red chilli
50ml/2 fl oz/scant ¼ cup water
salt, to taste
1 tsp dry-roasted cumin seeds
4 garlic cloves, peeled

Preparation 25 minutes + overnight soaking | **Cooking** 15 minutes | **Serves** 3–4

Soak the dried tamarind in the hot water overnight. The next day, squeeze the pulp with your hand and strain. For more on getting a good tamarind pulp, see p23.

Boil the red chillies in the measured water for 15 minutes, or until soft and squishy. Remove the chillies with a slotted spoon and place in a blender. Reserve the water.

Add the tamarind, salt, cumin and garlic to the blender with about 2 tablespoons of the reserved red chilli water and blend until smooth. If it is still thick, add the remaining chilli water. Transfer to a sterilised jar and use immediately or store the chutney in the fridge for up to a week.

Pomegranate and raspberry chutney
With black pepper and lime

Falsa season would be awaited with much anticipation when it arrived every summer. The tiny purple berries grow in Sindh and their flavour is a cross between the juiciness of raspberries and the tartness of pomegranate. They're unique and hard to get hold of – this chutney is a close recreation.

Preparation 15–20 minutes | **Serves** 3–4

1 punnet of raspberries
½ pomegranate, deseeded
½ tsp freshly ground
   black peppercorns
½ tsp kalanamak (black salt)
½ tsp dry-roasted cumin seeds
juice of ½ lime

Put the raspberries and pomegranate into a bowl and crush them using the back of a fork until mushy and the juice from the pomegranate mixes with the crushed raspberries.

Add the spices, the salt and the lime juice, and stir. Serve cold and eat within 24 hours.

Fresh mango pickle
With mustard seeds and mint

Sindhri mangos are as sweet as honey itself – which is probably why they go by the name 'honey mangos'. Most mango pickles are made with kayri (raw green mangos), but this recipe uses fresh ripe fruit (with a classic pickle spice mix), so it's best eaten fresh.

Preparation 15 minutes | **Cooking** 15 minutes | **Serves** 3–4

3 tbsp vegetable oil
1 tsp black mustard seeds
1 tsp fenugreek seeds
2 raw mango (kayri), chopped into
   tiny pieces (not to be confused with
   a full-grown, unripened mango,
   kayris can be found just before
   mango season (subsitute with
   ½ a ripened mango)
2 dried red chillies
1 tsp salt, or to taste
½ tsp ground turmeric
1 whole garlic clove, peeled
1 tsp tamarind paste (or homemade
   pulp, see p23)
2 tsp soft brown sugar
1–2 mint sprigs

Heat the oil in a frying pan with a lid over a low heat. When hot, add the mustard and fenugreek seeds, and as soon as they splutter, add the raw mango, dried red chillies, salt, turmeric and garlic. Stir–fry for about 2 minutes, or until the mango is slightly soft. Keep on a very low heat.

Add the tamarind and sugar, stir, then add the mint sprigs and turn the heat off. Cover the frying pan with a lid and allow the aroma of the mint to infuse with the rest of the ingredients for about 10 minutes.

This pickle is best enjoyed fresh and served at room temperature or can be stored for up to a week in the fridge. Remove the mint sprigs before serving.

Under a motia-filled sky
Celebration feasts

The atmosphere is thick with celebration: fragrant motia and rose bracelets adorn women dressed in festive attire, glass bangles clink together, glittery embellishments on dresses shine like stars. Then, in an instant, the aroma from the flowers is joined by the long-awaited smoke from barbecue pits, which rises to curl around the shimmering fairy lights, whispering of spice and slow cooking.

It's followed by saffron and sweet desserts scented with kewra water, a distilled extract of the pandanus flower. The very air carries the mouthwatering anticipation that fills everyone's mind at any celebration in Pakistan, be it Eid, a wedding or a festive dinner party.

Food takes centre stage in all Pakistani gatherings and festivals. I'm sure I remember people arriving right before meals were served at weddings, so as to avoid having to wait through the rituals before eating. Food would be cooked behind the scenes in massive steel cauldrons for hours before eventually being served at midnight, and people would pounce at it like hungry cats.

Our celebratory dinners are always big family affairs, with enormous sharing platters or buffet-style presentation; the dishes are rich, meaty and aromatic, and seemingly inexhaustible. Generosity and the enjoyment of food is the essence of the Pakistani 'dawwat' (feast).

All the recipes in this chapter are inspired by my memories of celebration: they require time and patience to create and should be served to your guests with the open arms of good hospitality.

Beef shami kebabs

This ultimate festive Pakistani kebab is actually pretty easy to make. minced beef is cooked with spices and chaana daal. It's then blended until almost a paste, formed into patties, and lightly fried. It's a dish from the kitchens of the Mughals, and nearly every Pakistani family has their own take on the heritage recipe.

450g/1lb/2 cups chana daal
1 kg/2¼ lb lean beef mince
   (ground beef)
2 medium onions, roughly cut
   into 4 pieces each
2 whole garlic cloves
1 long cinnamon quill
10–15 black peppercorns
6–8 cardamom pods, bruised
1 whole star anise
1 tbsp each of whole coriander
   (cilantro) seeds and cumin seeds
1 dried red chilli
2 bay leaves
salt, to taste
2 medium tomatoes, cut into 4
   pieces each
1 egg, beaten
4-cm/1½-inch piece ginger, peeled
1 small bunch of coriander (cilantro)
   leaves
2 green chillies, deseeded (optional)
½ bunch of mint leaves

Preparation 20 minutes + 30 minutes soaking | **Cooking** 1–1 hour 15 minutes | **Makes** 30

Soak the chana daal in a bowl of water for 30 minutes. Place all the ingredients, except the egg, ginger, herbs and green chilli, in a large saucepan with a lid. Pour in 700ml/24 fl oz/3 cups of water, or enough to cover the ingredients. Cook over a medium heat for 30–40 minutes until the water has evaporated – this is important as the mince needs to very dry when cooked. Keep stirring if required.

Once the mixture is bone dry (this is key), remove the solid spices (cinnamon, peppercorns, cardamom, star anise, chilli and bay leaves) and blitz the mince with the ginger in a food processor to a smooth paste. Add the beaten egg and blitz again to combine. Add the finely chopped coriander, chilli and mint.

To make the shami kebabs, mould 2 tablespoons of the mince into a golf ball-sized balls then flatten into a burger shape. Heat the oil in a shallow pan over a medium heat and fry the kebabs in batches for 2–3 minutes on each side until brown. Remove and drain on kitchen paper.

Kitchen secret

If the kebab seems to break up while cooking, dip them into a little flour then dip in beaten egg and fry. These kebabs freeze brilliantly for up to a month. Defrost them on a kitchen towel (this will absorb the moisture). Then dip in egg and shallow fry until hot through.

Hibiscus and Himalayan pink salt raita

Summer would bring luscious hibiscus flowers blooming in the garden, but I wouldn't be allowed to pick them lest I destroy my grandmother's hard work. Here I've combined dried petals with the minerality of pink salt. The result is stunning flavour and colour that looks regal on a dining table.

Preparation 10 minutes | **Serves** up to 6 people

Mix the yogurt, cumin and pink salt together in a bowl. Sprinkle over the hibiscus flower petals and allow the colour to seep through into the yogurt, then stir. Garnish with chillies and serve cool. It's the perfect accompaniment to the Sindhi biryani (see p160).

500g/1lb 2oz/2 cups whole Greek-style yogurt, whipped with a fork

1 tsp dry-roasted cumin seeds, crushed roughly in a mortar and pestle

1½ tsp ground Himalayan pink salt, or to taste

2 tsp dried hibiscus flowers, lightly pounded in a mortar and pestle

2 green finger chillies, deveined and finely chopped

Mutanjan
Rainbow sweet rice with candied fruits and saffron

This colourful sweet rice dish is traditionally served on festive days, either as a dessert, snack or before meals as a starter. Saffron yeilds the yellow, and you can use other natural food colours for the rainbow effect. It's served with khoya (milk solids), but clotted cream is a lovely alternative.

Preparation 40 minutes | **Cooking** 20–25 minutes | **Serves** 5–6 people

Wash the rice, rinse and soak in a bowl of water for 25–30 minutes. Drain.

To par-boil the rice, pour 600ml/1 pint/2½ cups water into a large saucepan and bring to the boil, then add the lemon slices. Add the drained rice and par-boil for 3–4 minutes. Drain, discard the lemons and put the rice into a clean heavy-based saucepan. Set aside.

Heat another saucepan, add the butter or ghee and the cardamom seeds, and when the butter is melted and fragrant, add the sugar and the remaining water. Stir until thick, about 3–5 minutes. Turn off the heat, add the nuts, raisins, candied peel and coconut, and stir. Turn the heat back on and cook for 2 minutes.

Pour this sugar syrup on to the par-boiled rice and top with the glacé cherries. Pour the saffron on to the rice in one area, the red colour on another and the green colour in another, ensuring that they do not mix together. Cover the pan with foil firmly around the edges, tightly cover with the lid and cook over a low heat in its own steam for about 8–10 minutes, or until the moisture has evaporated and the rice is cooked through. Gently stir with a fork until the colours mix together.

Serve small portions (a little goes a long way!) hot with a spoonful of clotted cream.

250g/9oz/1¼ cups basmati rice (excellent quality)

750ml/1½ pints/3 cups water

2 lemon slices

50g/2oz/4 tbsp butter or 3 tbsp ghee (see p23)

6 green cardamom pods, seeds removed

150g/5½oz/¾ cup golden caster (superfine) sugar

4 tbsp blanched almonds

4 tbsp unsalted shelled pistachios

4 tbsp golden raisins

3 tbsp candied peel

4 tbsp desiccated (dry unsweetened) coconut

10 glacé (candied) cherries

½ tsp saffron threads soaked in 2 tbsp boiling water

½ tsp each of red and green natural food colour

1 tub clotted cream, to serve

Sindhi mutton biryani

With sour plums and dried pomegranate

Sindhi biryani is by far the most aromatic and spicy biryani in this book, though the addition of potatoes, sour dried plums and dried pomegranate takes the edge off. This dish should take centre stage on the celebratory dining table, and while the ingredients list is long and it must be cooked with dedication, it's such a wonderful and worthwhile dish to make for a special occasion. Traditionally the rice and curry is layered twice, but I find that once is enough.

3–4 large potatoes, peeled and cut
    into thick chunks
50ml/2 fl oz/scant ¼ cup
    vegetable oil
6 green cardamom pods
2 black cardamom pods
1 cinnamon stick
2 bay leaves
2 tsp each of coriander (cilantro)
    seeds and black cumin
    (or cumin) seeds
1 tsp aniseed or fennel seeds
2 star anise
1 piece of mace
4 medium red onions, finely chopped
2 tsp each of grated ginger and
    crushed garlic
1kg/2¼lb mutton leg, cut into
    chunks, with bone
5 tomatoes, roughly chopped
1 tsp ground turmeric
1 tbsp ground anardana (dried
    pomegranate)
salt, to taste
10–15 dried plums (aloo bukharas)
2 green chillies chopped
200g/7oz/scant 1 cup Greek yogurt

For the rice
350g/12oz/1¾ cups basmati rice

To steam
1 tbsp kewra (screwpine water) or
    rose water
2 large pinches of saffron threads
1 tbsp ghee (see p23)
1 lemons, cut into slices
a few mint leaves

Preparation 45 minutes + 1 hour soaking | **Cooking** about 1 hour 15 minutes | **Serves** 8–10

Par-boil the potatoes in a large saucepan until par-cooked, then drain. Set aside.

Wash the rice, rinse and soak it in a bowl of water for 1 hour, then drain and par-boil for 3–4 minutes and drain. Soak the saffron threads in another bowl of hot milk for 15 minutes.

Heat the oil in a saucepan with a lid over a medium heat. Add the whole spices and allow to splutter. Add the onions and cook for 8–10 minutes until light brown. Add the ginger and garlic paste and cook until the raw smell disappears. Add the mutton and fry until it is sealed all over. Add the tomatoes, turmeric, dried pomegranate powder, salt, dried plums and green chilli and cook over a medium-high heat, stirring constantly for about 10 minutes, or until the oil rises to the top and the tomatoes are soft.

Add the yogurt and cook for about 10–15 minutes, stirring constantly, until the oil rises to the surface of the curry. Cover with a lid and cook for a further 10 minutes. You should be left with a thick curry with oil rising on the top. If it gets too thick then add a few splashes of water and reduce the heat to low until the oil rises back on the top. Add the par-boiled potatoes; at this point the meat should also be cooked through.

Layer the par-boiled rice on top of the meat in the pan then sprinkle the kewra, saffron and ghee over the top. Add lemon slices and mint. Cover the pan with foil firmly around the edges, cover tightly with the lid, reduce the heat to low, and let it cook in its own steam for about 10–15 minutes. If you have a heat diffuser it will help the rice steam evenly. The key is that when you remove the foil, steam should rise to the top and the rice should be standing on end. Anything further and the rice will be overcooked.

When ready, using a dessertspoon, stir the rice into the layers carefully so not to break the rice. Serve hot with a simple raita, such as hibiscus and Himalayan pink salt raita (see p159).

White chicken korma

With almond and pistachio

Most kormas in Pakistan are a rich reddish colour; however, this recipe of my mother's is a creamy white nutty version. This is not because of any addition of cream (using cream in kormas is uncommon in Pakistan), but because of the yogurt. Dried methi leaves added at the end gives the dish an unusual scent that's as intoxicating as it is haunting.

115g/4oz/¾ cup blanched almonds

3 tbsp ghee (see p23)

3 tbsp vegetable oil

1 cinnamon stick

5 green cardamom pods, crushed

2 large red onions, very finely chopped

1 tsp each of grated ginger and crushed garlic

4–5 tbsp vegetable or sunflower oil

1 kg/2¼ lb chicken, skinned and cut into 14 pieces

350ml/12 fl oz/1½ cups plain yogurt

2–3 dried long red chillies

salt, to taste

2 tbsp ground pistachios

½ tbsp dried methi (fenugreek) leaves

Preparation 15 minutes | **Cooking** 45–55 minutes | **Serves** 6–8

Put the almonds in a bowl of water and leave to soak. Heat the ghee and oil in a saucepan over a medium heat. Add the cinnamon and cardamon. When they splutter, add the onions and sauté for 5–6 minutes until soft. It is very important that the onions don't change colour at all, but are just allowed to get slightly translucent.

Add the ginger and garlic and stir-fry until the raw smell of garlic disappears. Do not let the mixture brown.

Heat some oil in a separate pan. When hot, add the chicken pieces and fry until they are a golden colour all over. Add the chicken to the onion mixture and continue to cook. At this point add the yogurt and bhuno (stir-fry) for a bit. Add the red chillies but make sure they don't break up, as it is vital that the korma does not get coloured by the chillies. I usually remove the seeds and add them later. Add salt to taste.

Meanwhile, blend the almonds with their soaking water to a smooth paste, then add to the pan together with the pistachios. Cover the pan with foil firmly around the edges, cover with the lid, reduce the heat to medium-low, and let it cook in its own steam. Keep checking on the korma. The end result should be a thick gravy. If it is watery, uncover, increase the heat to high heat and cook until the korma gravy is thick.

When the chicken is cooked and the gravy is ready, crush the dried methi between your hands and sprinkle over the top.

Kunna gosht

Slow-cooked lamb shank curry

Kunna gosht is a dish that will be familiar to those who have had nihari – it's very similar, but there's a subtle variation in spice. Hailing from the Punjabi town of Chinot (known for its beautiful hand-carved rosewood furniture), this rich and extravagant Punjabi wedding dish is made of slow-cooked lamb or mutton shanks and garam masalas. It's eaten topped with ginger, coriander leaves and more spice, and served alongside hot naans (see p58) or sheermal (see p169).

For the kunna

4 tbsp vegetable oil

2 tbsp ghee (see p23)

I large onion, thinly chopped

2.5-cm/1-inch piece ginger, peeled and finely grated

½ tbsp crushed garlic

2 kg/4½ lb leg of lamb chopped into 5–6 pieces with marrow exposed, or 3 large lamb shanks, cut into 2, marrow exposed

I tsp red chilli powder

2 tsp salt, or to taste

1½ tbsp Kashimri chilli powder

I litre/1¾ pints/4 cups water

2 tbsp plain (all-purpose) flour, mixed in a little water to form a paste

For the garam masala, grind together

I tbsp aniseed

2 large black cardamom pods

I cinnamon stick

10–12 green cardamom pods

2 star anise

I tbsp each of coriander (cilantro) seeds and cumin seeds (or 2 tsp black cumin seeds if available)

I piece of mace

10 cloves

10 black peppercorns

To garnish

large handful of coriander (cilantro)

5cm/2-inch piece ginger, peeled and cut into julienne

4 thin green chillies, finely chopped

4 large lemons, cut into wedges

10 medium onions, deep-fried until medium brown

Preparation 30 minutes | **Cooking** 3½ hours | **Serves** 10–12

Grind all the ingredients for the garam masala in a spice grinder. Set aside.

Heat the oil and ghee together in a pan over a medium heat. When hot, add the onion, ginger and garlic and cook for a few minutes, stirring until the raw smell disappears. Add the lamb and fry until the meat is sealed. Add the red chilli powder, salt and about 3–4 tablespoons of the ground garam masala, reserving 2–3 tablespoons as a garnish. Fry until the masala is fragrant. If it is sticking to the pan add a splash of water as you go. Add the Kashimiri chilli powder and stir until the meat is evenly coated in all the masalas.

Pour in the measured water to cover the meat. You may need to add more water to ensure the meat is completely covered. Reduce the heat slightly to medium-low. Cover and cook for about 45 minutes to I hour. Keep checking to make sure that the meat is not overboiling. After about an hour, remove 240ml/8 fl oz/I cup of the liquid from the meat and beat into it the flour paste. Now pour it back into the main saucepan and stir in evenly. Add the reserved 240ml/8 fl oz/I cup water, then cover with the lid, reduce the heat to very low and cook gently for 2 hours, or until the meat falls off the bone.

Serve hot topped with coriander, the remaining garam masala and finely julienned ginger, chopped green chillies, lemon wedges and deep-fried onions in small bowls on the side. Enjoy with naan (see p58), crusty bread, rice or sheermal (see p169).

Beef kitchra
Lentil, barley and oat stew

Kitchra is a festive and satisfying dish which is cooked on religious holidays. This is a one-pot meal, made with chicken, beef or mutton on the bone, together with simple spices and cereals. It takes patience to prepare, but the results are rewarding. On religious holidays, kitchra or haleem is made and given to the poor and needy — queues form outside generous homes, where steaming bowls of meat stew with naans are given out in large helpings.

30g/1oz/scant ¼ cup each moong daal, urid daal and chana daal

250g/9oz/scant 1¼ cups pearl barley or wheatgerm

1kg/2¼lb braising or chuck steak, cut into chunks

2 tsp each of crushed ginger and garlic

1 cinnamon stick

2 star anise

2 black cardamom pods

1 tsp ground turmeric

1 tsp crushed dried red chilli

2 litres/3½ pints/8 cups water

20g/¾ oz/¼ cup rolled oats

5 tbsp vegetable oil

1 red onion, cut into slices

For the condiments

2 red onions, thinly cut, fried in oil until brown, then drained

1 bunch of fresh tender coriander, (cilantro) with stems, chopped

½ bunch of mint, leaves only and finely chopped

2.5cm/1-inch piece ginger, peeled and cut into julienne

1 tbsp garam masala (see p26)

3 green chillies, finely chopped

2 lemons, cut into wedges

Preparation 30 minutes + soaking overnight | **Cooking** 3 hours | **Serves** 10–12

Soak all the lentils and barley in water overnight. The next day, drain and place in a heavy-based saucepan with a lid with the beef chunks, ginger, garlic and all the spices. Pour in the water, bring to the boil and remove any scum that forms on the surface with a slotted spoon. Reduce the heat, partially cover and cook for up to 2 hours, checking the water frequently and stirring to make sure it's not sticking to the base of the pan. It should begin to resemble a thick porridge with chunks of meat. The lentils should be soft and the meat can be mashed with the back of a spoon.

Add the oats and cook for another 10 minutes. When cooked, turn the heat off and cover with the lid.

Heat the oil in a small frying pan over a medium heat. When hot, add the onions and cook for 8–10 minutes until brown. Pour this over the kitchra and cover with a lid.

To serve, pour out a portion per person into a bowl and arrange all the condiments in small bowls, adding a little of each to every serving. Try serving with sheermal (see p169).

Sheermal

Semi-sweet saffron and cardamom-enriched bread

This saffron-flavoured semi-sweet leavened bread has its roots in Persian and North Indian cooking. It's very much a festive bread that's a traditional accompaniment to kunna gosht (p165) or kitchra (see p166). They can be made in advance and they freeze very well – to defrost, simply toast.

210g/7oz/1 cup strong bread flour

½ tsp salt

1½ tbsp caster (superfine) sugar

½ tsp fast-action (active dry) yeast

4 tbsp milk powder

½ tsp ground cardamom

100ml/3½ fl oz/scant ½ cup whole milk

2 tbsp hot milk infused with ½ tsp saffron threads

3 tbsp ghee or melted unsalted butter, plus extra for greasing (see p23)

3 tbsp double (heavy) cream

1 egg

lukewarm water, for binding

½ tsp rose water or kewra water (screwpine extract)

milk, for brushing

1 tsp sesame seeds, poppy seeds, nuts

Preparation 15 minutes + 1½ hours rising | **Cooking** 15 minutes | **Makes** 4–5

Place all the dry ingredients in a bowl, add the remaining ingredients and mix to make a soft dough. Cover and allow to rise in a warm place for 1½ hours.

Remove the dough from the bowl and place on a lightly floured work surface. Punch the dough down to get rid of excessive air, then knead for 7–10 minutes.

Preheat the oven to 200°C/400°F/gas mark 6 and grease a baking tray with ghee or butter. Make 4–6 round balls from the dough and cover with a piece of clingfilm.

Flatten the balls with the palm of your hands then roll out into rounds. Turn and flatten to about 3–4 mm/⅛ inch thick. Use a fork to pierce the rounds all over then brush with 3 tablespoons milk and sprinkle with poppy seeds, sesame or nuts. Place on the baking tray.

Put the baking tray on the middle shelf of the oven and bake for 12–15 minutes until golden and puffed. Turn over and cook for a further 2 minutes until light brown. Remove from the oven, brush with a little more milk and keep in foil until ready to eat.

Slow-cooked chana daal
Topped with daal dust

A favourite for festive meals. Chana daal cooks best if soaked overnight and then boiled. Cook until the daal is soft yet still maintains its shape, and dry out all the moisture before tempering.

150g/5oz/1½ cups chana daal
1 garlic clove
1 tsp red chili powder
½ tsp ground turmeric
1 cinnamon stick
salt, to taste
1 tbsp ghee (see p23)
5 garlic cloves, sliced
1 tsp cumin seeds
2 long dried red chillies
5–6 curry leaves (fresh if possible)
1 onion, thinly sliced, fried until
    brown then rested on kitchen
    paper
½ bunch of coriander (cilantro)
2.5-cm/1-inch piece ginger, peeled
    and cut into julienne
1 tsp chaat masala (see p26)
1 tsp garam masala and 'daal dust'
    (see p26)
2 tbsp tamarind sauce (see p23)

Preparation 10 minutes + overnight soaking | **Cooking** 30–40 minutes | **Serves** 5–6

Soak the chana daal in a bowl of water overnight. The next day, drain and put into a large saucepan with the garlic, red chilli powder, turmeric and cinnamon stick. Pour in 350ml/ 12 fl oz/1½ cups water, or enough to cover the daal and bring to the boil. Cook for 15–20 minutes until the daal is soft. You are looking for a firm and not mushy daal. You may need to top up the water every now and then. Once the daal is cooked, add salt.

In a small frying or tarka pan, heat the ghee over a medium heat until melted then add the sliced garlic; when it starts to brown lightly, add the cumin, dried red chillies and curry leaves and cook for about 10 seconds, or until they splutter.

Put the daal in a serving bowl then pour the tarka over. Garnish with coriander, ginger, chaat masala (see p26), daal dust (see p26) and tamarind sauce (see p23).

Kashmiri-style leg of lamb

Roasted with almonds, coconut and rose

This is a recipe that reminds me of the cool, crisp Karachi winters and the festivities that they bring. The lamb is always slow-cooked in a pot, and resonates with the flavours of Kashmir: the sweetness of raisins, the warmth of nuts, the headiness of spice. This is my take on a dish that represents both Kashmiri respect for food and the togetherness of mealtimes.

150g/5½oz/⅔ cup plain yogurt
3 tbsp vegetable oil
juice of 1 lemon
2 kg/4½ lb leg of lamb

For the whole spices

2.5cm/1-inch cinnamon stick
6 whole cloves
10green cardamom pods
1½ tsp coriander (cilantro) seeds
1 tsp black peppercorns
1 small piece of mace
1 dried Kashmiri chilli or 2 tsp
  Kashmiri chilli powder
1 tsp aniseed
2 tbsp dried edible rose petals

For the marinade

1½ tsp garlic paste
1½ tsp ginger paste
2 tbsp desiccated (dry unsweetened)
  coconut
3 tbsp ground almonds
1 tbsp white poppy seeds
1 large red onion, browned and
  ground into a paste in a food
  processor

Preparation 30 minutes + 1–2 hours marinating | **Cooking** 1–2 hours | **Serves** 10

Blitz all the marinade ingredients in a blender until a paste forms. Transfer to a bowl. Grind all the spices into a spice grinder to a powder. Add the yogurt to the marinade paste with the ground spices and vegetable oil and mix together.

Rub the lemon juice all over the leg of lamb then, using a sharp knife, cut the lamb all over with 5cm/2-inch slits. Cover the lamb all over with the marinade, rubbing it into the slits, then cover and allow to marinate for 1–2 hours, or overnight if possible.

Heat a large ovenproof pan. When hot, add the lamb and cook until it is sealed on all sides. Add the water together with any remaining marinade and cook over a medium heat for up to 2 hours, depending on how you like the meat.

You can also bake the lamb in an oven preheated to 180°C/350°F/gas mark 4 for 2–3 hours, uncovered for the first 15 minutes then covered with foil for the remaining time.

Once ready, remove the lamb from the pan and allow to rest for 15–20 minutes before carving and serving with any of the juices left in the pan.

Mummy's festive minty beef kofta curry

Every family in Pakistan has a secret kofta (meatball) curry recipe. Many families guard these, others are happy to share. My mother taught me how to get the koftas beautifully soft without them breaking apart while cooking, and the addition of mint in her original recipe adds a flavour that other kofta curries lack.

For the koftas

500g/1lb 2oz beef mince
(ground beef)
1 slice of bread, soaked in water
and then squeezed
4 tbsp brown onion paste
(To make: slice 3 red onions and
fry until lightly brown, then grind
into a paste in a blender with about
3–4 tbsp water)
1 tbsp chickpea flour
1 tsp freshly ground coriander
(cilantro) seeds
½ tsp freshly ground cumin seeds
1 tsp garam masala (see p26)
¾ tsp red chilli powder
1–1½ tsp salt, or to taste
1 tsp ginger and garlic paste
small handful of coriander (cilantro),
finely chopped
2–3 mint leaves, finely chopped
1 green chilli, finely chopped
(optional)

For the curry

2–3 tbsp vegetable oil
2 tbsp brown onion paste (as above)
½ tsp red chilli powder
1 tsp Kashmiri chilli powder
1 tsp salt, or to taste
½ tsp ground turmeric
1 tsp freshly ground coriander
(cilantro) seeds
1 tsp freshly ground cumin seeds
2 tbsp white poppy seeds
4 tbsp plain yogurt
600ml/1 pint/2½ cups water
10–12 mint leaves, torn

Preparation 45 minutes | **Cooking** 45–55 minutes | **Serves** 6–10

Using only 2 tablespoons of the onion paste (reserve rest for the curry), mince all the ingredients for the koftas, except the coriander, mint and green chilli, then stir them in last. Roll about 1 heaped tablespoon of the mince into medium-sized meatballs (not too small) and make sure that there are no cracks in them. Set aside. The meatballs are added in raw, as they cook in the curry.

To make the curry, heat the oil in a shallow pan with a lid over a medium heat. When hot, add the remaining onion paste and fry for 1 minute. Add the red chilli powder, Kashmiri chilli powder, salt and a splash of water and cook for 10–15 minutes until the oil rises to the surface and a red colour develops in the curry. Add the turmeric, coriander, cumin and another splash of water and cook for 10–12 minutes until the oil separates and the curry turns red.

Add the poppy seeds and cook for about 2–3 minutes. Add the yogurt and fry until the oil separates and the curry is cooked through. Pour in the water, then the raw meatballs (add more water if you wish the curry to be thin). Reduce the heat to medium-low, cover with the lid and cook for about 15–20 minutes, or until the meatballs are cooked.

Finally, add the torn mint leaves. Cover the pan and turn off the heat. Serve with a few extra torn mint leaves and enjoy with either plain basmati rice or fresh hot naan (see p58).

Khubani ka meetha

Hunza apricots with custard and cream

Hunza apricots have a stunning toffee-like flavour and this Hyderabadi dessert is a little taste of heaven. The unassuming dried fruit is rehydrated overnight in water then stewed and served with a rich, creamy custard. This recipe was shared with me by my old friend Humaira.

1kg/2¼lb Hunza apricots
250g/9oz/1¼ cups caster
(superfine) sugar
250g/9oz ready-made vanilla custard
(shop-bought custard works best)
250g/9oz/1 cup double (heavy)
cream, whipped
1 tbsp blanched dry-roasted almonds,
to decorate (optional)

Preparation 30 minutes + overnight soaking | **Cooking** 1 hour 20 minutes | **Serves** 8–10

The day before making the dessert, wash the dried apricots and soak them in a bowl of water overnight. The water should come up 3 fingers or 5cm/2 inches above the apricots. Leave the bowl uncovered.

The next day, the apricots should have doubled in size and become plump. Remove the stones carefully without breaking the flesh. Reserve the stones and the water.

In the same water, boil the stoned apricots for about 30 minutes over a medium-low heat without stirring too much, so the apricots don't go mushy, until all the water has evaporated.

Reduce the heat to low, add the sugar, without stirring too much again, and allow the sugar to dissolve and form a syrup. This takes about 5–10 minutes. Switch off the heat. The texture should be thick, pulpy and sticky. Cover the pan with a sieve, to allow the apricots to cool and protect them from anything falling into them.

As soon as they are completely cold, place them in the fridge, or freeze until ready to use.

When ready to serve, put the apricots into individual serving dishes, add a layer of custard then a layer of whipped cream.

Traditionally, this dessert is decorated with the nuts found inside the stone of the Hunza apricot, which can be easily removed, if gently bashed out. Alternatively, decorate with blanched, dry-roasted almonds.

Double ka meetha
Hyderbadi-style saffron bread pudding

Double roti is the Urdu name for a loaf of plain bread, which is the star ingredient of this exotic bread pudding. A modest slice of bread is infused with creamy saffron milk and topped with pistachios and silver leaf to create a truly celebratory dessert.

500ml/17 fl oz/2 cups whole milk
3 cardamom pods, seeds removed
    and crushed, husks discarded
3 tbsp condensed milk
50ml/2 fl oz/scant ¼ cup double
    (heavy) cream
200g/7oz/scant 1 cup ricotta cheese
½ tsp crushed saffron threads
100g/3½oz/½ cup caster
    (superfine) sugar
100ml/3½ fl oz/½ cup water
3–4 tbsp ghee or butter mixed with
    2 tbsp vegetable oil (see p23)
10 slices plain white bread,
    crusts off and cut into half
    diagonally (2 triangles)
1 tbsp chopped nuts
1 tbsp rose petals
1 tbsp silver leaf

Preparation 15–20 minutes | **Cooking** 35–40 minutes | **Serves** 10–14

Preheat the oven to 170°C/338°F/gas mark 3. Bring the whole milk with the cardamom to the boil in a saucepan. Once it reaches the boil, reduce the heat and simmer for 15 minutes, or until the milk reduces and thickens slightly.

Add the condensed milk and double cream and stir through. Ladle out about 2 tablespoons of the hot milk and place in a bowl with the ricotta. Mix together, then pour back into the hot milk and stir. Add the saffron and stir. Leave on a very low heat while making the sugar syrup.

In another saucepan make the sugar syrup. Heat the sugar with the water over a medium heat for about 4–5 minutes, or until a thin syrup is formed. Remove the pan from the heat and set aside.

Heat the ghee in a frying pan. When hot, add the bread and lightly fry each side until golden brown, adding more ghee if it gets absorbed. Keep placing each slice of fried bread into the syrup for a few seconds and then place in a ovenproof serving dish side by side. Pour the milk mixture evenly over the bread.

Bake the dessert in the oven for 10–12 minutes, or until light brown around the edges and on top. Serve hot or chill in the fridge and serve cold decorated with chopped nuts, rose petals and silver leaf.

The sweet taste of mango heaven

Desserts

My childhood was one of sweetness and spice. Whether it was a reward of a saffron-drenched jalebi, a rosewater-laced gulab jaman or a cardamom-flavoured, fudge-like barfi, I always found comfort in Pakistani sweets and desserts.

There's a difference in the way we eat our sweets in Pakistan. Our 'meetha' (desserts) can accompany a cup of chai at teatime, and 'meethai' (sweetmeats) serve as a treat to mark a festive occasion. Those gulab jamans on restaurant menus seem to me but appendages, as it's not usual to end a meal with rich, milky, syrup-drenched puddings. And most meals in Pakistan end with an array of cut seasonal fruit: summer sees mangos, falsas and kino oranges, while in winter we have apples, pomegranates, chickoo, apricots and guava.

But there's no denying the fact: in Pakistan we do have a real love affair with sweets. The sighting of the moon as Eid begins, rejoicing a birth, welcoming a bride into her new home… nearly every occasion of happiness involves a distribution of sweetmeats like ladoo and barfi.

Sweet and savoury are also not separated to the same extent as they are in the West. We find ways to infuse our sweets with spices, such as korma mixed with sweet zarda rice, or semolina halva with hot chickpeas and puri for breakfast (see p29). Our taste buds love both flavour sensations together, and so if something is to be sweet it must be very sweet. This might be why you can't take the sweet tooth out of a Pakistani, no matter where they go.

Enjoy these dessert recipes – some modern, others traditional – with a cup of chai, or after a meal if you need that sweet ending as much as me.

Mango and chilli papper
Oven-dried fruit roll-ups

The addition of dried red chilli flakes makes these dehydrated mango fruit leathers deliciously moreish – and a challenge to eat when the heat kicks in rather unexpectedly. You can make these in a dehydrator if you have one, however it works perfectly on a very low temperature in the oven. This is more of a treat than a dessert.

2 large mangos, preferably Pakistani honey mangos or any other sweet ripe mangos, cored and cut into chunks
½ tsp sea salt
½ tsp red chilli flakes
½ tbsp honey

Preparation 20 minutes | **Cooking** 4–5 hours | **Serves** 5–8

Preheat the oven to 55–65°C/131–149°F/lowest possible gas mark and line a baking sheet with parchment paper.

Purée the mango pieces in a blender to a thick consistency, then add the salt, chilli and honey.

Pour the fruit mixture on to the prepared baking sheet – it should be about 3mm/ ⅛-inch thick. Bake in the oven for 4–6 hours, or until the leather peels away easily from the parchment paper. Using scissors, cut the leather into long rectangular shapes and roll them up with the leftover parchment to stop them from sticking to any surface until you are ready to eat them.

Store in a cool, dry and airtight container and eat within 5–6 days.

Saffron chana daal halva
With cloves and cardamom

You would be hard pressed to find something that Pakistanis don't tend to churn into halva. This is a classic lentil halva made by my mother. It has a surprisingly simple flavour, though is a little laborious to make. It can be formed into balls, cut into squares and served warm or at room temperature.

200g/7oz/scant 1 cup chana daal
1 litre/1¾ pints/2½ cups whole milk
4 tbsp ghee (see p23)
2–4 cardamom pods, crushed,
    use seeds only
200g/7oz/1 cup caster (superfine)
    sugar
a generous pinch of saffron threads,
    crushed in a mortar and pestle and
    soaked in 1 tbsp hot milk

To garnish
handful of slivered pistachios, flaked
    (slivered) almonds and silver leaf

Preparation 15 minutes + overnight soaking | **Cooking** 40–50 minutes | **Serves** 6–10

Soak the chana daal overnight in a bowl of water. The next day, drain the daal and boil with the milk in a saucepan for 20–25 minutes, stirring constantly until the daal is tender, the milk is absorbed and the mixture is dryish. Place the mixture into a food processor and blitz to a very well-blended dry paste. Set aside.

Heat the ghee in another saucepan over a medium heat and add the cardamon seeds and cook until the ghee is fragrant. Add the lentil paste and fry, moving the mixture around constantly over a medium-low heat for 5–8 minutes until the mixture smells very nutty and the colour is light brown. Make sure you keep moving the mixture around to prevent it from burning.

In another saucepan, make a thin sugar syrup. With enough water to cover the sugar, heat over a medium heat for about 4–5 minutes, or until a thin syrup is formed. Remove from the heat and pour the sugar syrup directly over the lentil mixture (keeping over a low heat) and mix and cook for a few minutes. Add the saffron and mix this very quickly so it doesn't cool or harden.

Remove from the heat and pour it into a dish. Allow to cool slightly before either making into small cylindrical shapes or placing it into a flat dish and scoring the mixture with a knife into diamond shapes.

Allow to cool and decorate with the nuts and silver leaf. Eat at room temperature. This keeps for about 3–5 days covered in a cool, dry place.

Gulab jamans
Infused with Earl Grey tea

On the day my Dadi (paternal grandmother) migrated to Pakistan in 1947, she made gulab jamans, and took no other perishables from her home. Once across the border, biting into one brought bittersweet memories as she tasted home in the new land in which she was to live forever. She says that bite marked the end of a previous life and the beginning of a new one. I've combined an English tea with the sweet syrup, giving these gulab jamans a taste of my life in Britain.

For the gulab jaman balls

2–3 tbsp of Earl Grey tea infusion (made from 3–4 teabags)
2 tsp semolina (suji)
2½ tbsp self-raising flour
50g/1¾ oz whole milk powder
2–3 tsp ghee (see p23)
2 tbsp whole milk
2 tbsp ghee and 500ml/17 fl oz/ 2 cups vegetable oil, for deep-frying the jamans

For the sugar syrup

100g/3½ oz/½ cup caster (superfine) sugar
7–10 cardamom pods, seeds removed
600ml/1 pint/2½ cups water
50ml/2 fl oz/scant ¼ cup Earl Grey tea infusion (see method)
a large pinch of saffron threads
1 tbsp rose water

Preparation 40 minutes + 5–8 hours chilling | **Cooking** 30–40 minutes | **Serves** 7–8

To make the Earl Grey tea infusion, soak the teabags in a cup of boiling water, then cool and chill for 5 hours, or overnight.

Place all the ingredients for the sugar syrup in a saucepan over a medium heat and cook until everything has dissolved and the syrup boils. Reduce the heat and cook gently for about 5 minutes to form a thin sugar syrup.

Next, make the gulab jamans. Mix all the dry ingredients in a bowl then add the ghee and milk and tea infusion, a bit at a time, until a crumbly dough forms and all the ingredients stick together. At this point remove the dough from the bowl and knead on a clean work surface until smooth. Return the dough to the bowl and cover with clingfilm.

Heat the ghee and oil mixture in a large pan over a low heat. The trick is to keep the heat low and the oil/ghee mixture not too hot. This should not be so hot it burns the outside, yet hot enough to allow it to cook the inside completely.

Form small balls (I tend to make them small as they double up and are easier and faster to cook) with the dough and pop them into the hot ghee and oil. Do not overcrowd the pan: you should let them free float and cook evenly on all sides. Once they are medium brown and puffed up, remove them with a slotted spoon and drop them immediately into the sugar syrup. Keep doing this until all the jamans are ready. When cut open, the jamans should be moist, gooey and cooked through. To serve, remove the jamans from the sugar syrup.

Walnut and cardamom ladoo

Walnuts grow in abundance in northern Pakistan, and this is a traditional dessert making use of the bounty.

2 tbsp ghee (see p23)

3 green cardamom pods, seeds finely ground

250g/9oz/2½ cups shelled walnuts, finely ground

150–200ml/5–7 fl oz/⅔–scant 1 cup condensed milk

3 tbsp desiccated (dry unsweetened) coconut

Preparation 15 minutes | **Cooking** 15 minutes | **Serves** 6–8

Heat the ghee in a heavy-based saucepan over a medium heat. When hot, add the ground cardamom and stir for 2–3 minutes until the ghee is fragrant. Add the ground walnuts and stir for about 2 minutes until the walnuts smell slightly roasted.

Pour in the condensed milk and stir vigorously for about 10 minutes or so, or until the mixtures comes together like a ball. Once you reach this stage, turn off the heat and allow the walnut mixture to cool for about 3–4 minutes.

Spread the desiccated coconut out on a plate. Using your hands, form about 1 tablespoon of the mixture into a golf ball-sized balls then roll in the desiccated coconut. Place on a plate and allow to cool completely.

Cover and store in a cool, dry place and eat within 3–4 days.

Semolina brittle
Topped with pistachio and sea salt

My Dadi's (paternal grandmother) recipe for these sweets are an unusual way to use semolina. You can top these with pistachios and sea salt as I have, or any nuts you like. The trick is to score the semolina quickly, as the sugar syrup hardens almost instantly, a bit like peanut brittle.

2–3 tbsp ghee, plus extra for greasing (see p23)
2–3 cardamom pods, ground
250g/9oz/1½ cups fine semolina
250–300g/9–10½ oz/1¼–1½ cups caster (superfine) sugar
½ tsp saffron threads
about 25ml/1 fl oz/2 tbsp water
2 tbsp finely sliced pistachios
½ tsp Maldon salt

Preparation 15 minutes | **Cooking** 10 minutes | **Serves** 7–8

Line a baking tray with parchment paper and grease with ghee then set aside.

Heat the ghee in a saucepan over a medium heat, then add the ground cardamom and semolina and stir for 2 minutes until aromatic: do not allow to brown. Remove from the heat and set aside.

In another saucepan, add the sugar, saffron and 500ml/17 fl oz/2 cups of water, or enough to just cover the sugar. Bring to the boil and cook for about 3–4 minutes until it becomes a thin sugar syrup. Remove from the heat.

Stir the semolina into the syrup and stir vigorously. This should be a pourable consistency. Pour the semolina on to the prepared baking tray and spread out until it is 5mm/¼ inch thick. Scatter the pistachios and salt evenly over the top. Using a knife, score the semolina quickly as it dries really fast. Make into triangles, diamonds or whatever shape you like.

Allow to dry for 20 minutes then peel the pieces off the parchment paper.

Nani's firni

Screwpine-infused ground rice pudding

A classic Pakistani dessert, usually made in tiny, shallow, unglazed terracotta bowls which infuse the ground rice with their earthy essence. The authentic taste of this comforting dessert comes from the addition of cardamom and screwpine water (you can use rose water in its place). Nearly all nights spent at my Nani's (maternal grandmother) house would result in her being coerced into making firni – hers was always the most delicious, and full of her unconditional love.

60g/2¼ oz ground rice
200ml/7 fl oz/scant 1 cup water
500ml/17 fl oz/2 cups whole milk
100g/3½ oz/scant ½ cup caster
   (superfine) sugar
200ml/7 fl oz/ scant 1 cup
   condensed milk
4 tbsp ricotta cheese
½ tsp ground cardamom
a pinch of saffron threads
1 tsp kewra (screwpine extract)
   or rose water

To decorate
1 tbsp chopped pistachios
1 tbsp dried edible rose petals
1 tbsp edible silver leaf

Preparation 10 minutes | **Cooking** 15 minutes | **Serves** 6

In a bowl, soak the ground rice in the water. Bring the milk to the boil in a large saucepan over a medium heat. As soon as it is boiling, reduce the heat and simmer for 10 minutes, or until thick.

Add the sugar, condensed milk and the soaked ground rice to the milk and return to the boil. Let the milk boil for another 5–7 minutes, stirring constantly. It should start to thicken up now.

Add the ricotta and cardamom – this should now be the consistency of thick custard. Keep stirring to prevent it burning. Turn off the heat and stir in the saffron and rose water or kewra. Allow to cool for a few minutes before pouring the firni into terracotta or glass bowls and top with chopped pistachios.

Chill in the refrigerator for at least 1 hour before serving. Decorate with rose petals and silver leaf.

Sweet jaggery rice

With cloves and cardamom

This recipe for jaggery-infused rice came from Anwar Khala, my mother's sister, and was an everyday indulgence for my uncle. The nutty sweetness of jaggery (sugarcane molasses), together with the warmth of cloves and cardamom, makes a great finish to a spicy meal – though it's equally good eaten with a cup of tea.

200g/7oz/1 cup jaggery or muscovado sugar

about 250ml/9 fl oz/1 cup water

2 tsp aniseed

10 cloves

3–4 cardamom pods, seeds removed

1 tbsp ghee (see p23)

100g/3½oz/½ cup basmati rice, washed, soaked and drained

1 tbsp shelled pistachios

1 tbsp raisins

1 tbsp coconut slivers

100g/3½oz/scant ½ cup double (heavy) cream, to serve

Preparation 15 minutes | **Cooking** 30 minutes | **Serves** 4–5

Break the jaggery into small pieces and place in a large saucepan with the water, aniseed, cloves and cardamom seeds. Bring to the boil and boil for 5–7 minutes, or until the jaggery has dissolved.

In another saucepan with a lid, add the ghee and drained basmati rice. Fry for a few seconds over a medium heat then strain the sugar syrup over the rice to just cover the rice. Cover the saucepan with the lid, reduce the heat to low and cook for about 5–7 minutes. Keep checking if the rice is cooked through or the sugar is all absorbed. Add any remaining sugar syrup to cover the rice and cook through.

Once ready, the rice should be cooked and all the liquid should be dry. If you find that the rice is still wet, uncover and stir until done.

Decorate with pistachios, raisins and coconut and serve with double cream.

Peshawari falooda
Pistachio ice-cream float

Late-evening cravings for ice cream would lead to my father taking us out for falooda – an ice cream float decorated with a pink rose syrup called rooh afza, as well as puffy basil seeds and china grass noodles. Peshawari ice cream is famous all over the country: it's made from rich buffalo cream, and pistachio is my all-time favourite. The combination of rose, milk and pistachio pretty much sums up the flavour of all things sweet in Pakistan.

For the pistachio ice cream

2 litres/3½ pints/8 cups milk

500ml/17 fl oz/2 cups double (heavy) cream

1 heaped tsp ground cardamom

1 teaspoon gum mastic crystals, crushed with 1 teaspoon caster (superfine) sugar (optional)

100g/3½oz/½ cup caster (superfine) sugar

3 tsp kewra (screwpine water) or rose water

200ml/7 fl oz/scant 1 cup evaporated milk

50g/1¾oz/⅓ cup chopped pistachios

2–3 drops pistachio essence (optional)

3–5 drops natural green food colour

For the falooda

½ packet falooda china glass noodles

12 tbsp condensed milk

1 tbsp crushed pistachios

4 tsp soaked and drained basil seeds (see p203)

1 tbsp dried edible rose petals (optional)

2 tbsp rooh afza rose syrup (see p203)

mint leaves, to decorate

Preparation 35 minutes | **Cooking** 20 minutes + freezing time | **Serves** 4–6

Heat the milk and double cream in a saucepan over a medium-low heat. Once warm add the ground cardamom and bring to the boil. Reduce the heat and simmer for 25–30 minutes, stirring occasionally, until the liquid has reduced by about a quarter and it is a rich creamy colour. Turn off the heat and add the crushed mastic. Allow to cool in the fridge while you make the kewra syrup.

Into another saucepan, add the sugar and kewra and cook gently over a low heat until the sugar has dissolved and it becomes a thin syrup. Remove from the heat and cool.

Strain the milk and double cream liquid and discard the solids in the milk. Add the evaporated milk and combine with the kewra syrup, then add the pistachios, pistachio essence and green food colour and stir in gently to mix. Allow to cool then chill in the fridge for 15 minutes.

Churn the mixture in an ice-cream machine until it is thick enough to scoop. Alternatively, freeze the chilled mixture, whisking with a hand whisk or electric mixer every 30 minutes or so to prevent crystals forming. Repeat until it is frozen to a soft scoop consistency.

Soak the falooda noodles in a bowl of water for 10 minutes, then drain.

To assemble the falooda float, place a small handful of falooda noodles in a serving glass, pour over 3 tablespoons of condensed milk and a scoop or two of the pistachio cardamom ice cream. Top with crushed pistachios, 1 teaspoon soaked and drained basil seeds and a teaspoon of rose syrup (rooh afza). Decorate with mint leaves.

Nani's sheer khurma
Warm sweet vermicelli drink with dates, saffron and nuts

This is a warming drink with a texture that also makes it a great dessert. The milky goodness of ghee-tossed vermicelli, sat under warm saffron milk, chopped pistachios and chewy, sweet, dried dates, is a pure taste of Eid in Pakistan. You can have it at breakfast, offer it as a hospitable drink to guests or save it for an after dinner treat.

2 tbsp ghee (see p23)

4 green cardamom pods, seeds removed and crushed with a mortar and pestle

3 tbsp crushed fine wheat vermicelli (seviyan)

2 tbsp slivered pistachios

2 tbsp slivered almonds

1 tbsp green raisins

600ml/1 pint/2½ cups milk

½ can evaporated milk

50g/1¾ oz/¼ cup caster (superfine) sugar, or to taste

½ tsp crushed saffron threads

5 dried dates (choara) soaked in warm water overnight, then chopped into 4 pieces

Preparation 15 minutes | **Cooking** 20 minutes | **Serves** 5–6

Heat the ghee in a saucepan over a medium heat, then add the cardamom seeds and cook for 10–15 seconds until fragrant. Add the vermicelli and stir constantly for 5–7 minutes to avoid them turning too dark and burning

Add the nuts and raisins and cook for about 30 seconds. Add the whole milk followed by the evaporated milk and sugar. Reduce the heat to low and simmer until the vermicelli is cooked and the milk begins to thicken slightly. The consistency needs to resemble a milky drink, so if it gets too thick, add a little more milk.

Add the crushed saffron and chopped dates, warm through and allow the saffron to colour the milk. Turn the heat off and serve warm in small glasses.

Chai-pani
Hot and cold drinks

A cup of cardamom chai cures all woes.

In the same way the British love a 'cuppa', much of the fabric of Pakistani social culture revolves around the quintessential cup of tea. It brings people together as they take respite from the heat and find solace in a cup of slow-brewed chai.

'Chai-pani' is an expression with a dual meaning: it literally translates as 'tea and water', but is both a friendly invitation to a friend for a catch-up, and the repayment of a favour. With the promise of either a hot or cool drink, the meeting is sweeter, the favour is returned satisfactorily. No matter the sentiment, a 'garam' (warm) chai or a 'thandi' (cool) lassi soothes the Pakistani soul.

A memory that has never left me is one of makeshift roadside stoves brewing the Pathan chai of the people from the north of Pakistan, served in small enamel teapots and poured into glass tumblers. Hot days were made bearable with soothing warm chai, fresh buffalo milk lassi or 'dooth ki botel', a drink made with raw milk, ground nuts and poppy seeds.

This chapter brings together hot and cold beverages that tap into the emotions and flavours of Pakistan. Some are easy to make, others need a little work to source ingredients, but each brings with it a true taste of the country, one sip at a time.

Noon chai
Kashmiri-inspired pink tea

Big, hot cauldrons of this salty sweet pistachio-topped tea would brew for hours during the late-night festivities which are so common in Pakistan. The savoury-sweet flavour is an acquired taste – if you like it, it's best enjoyed as a nightcap, though it can be made without the salt if you prefer.

2 tsp Kashmiri tea leaves or
    pure green tea leaves (this is a
    family version, and can be
    substituted if Kashmiri tea leaves
    are not available)
350–475ml/12–16 fl oz/1½–2
    cups water
¼–½ tsp bicarbonate of soda
    (baking soda)
2–3 green cardamom pods, seeds
    removed and roughly crushed
1 litre/1¾ pints/4 cups whole milk
¼–½ tsp sea salt OR sugar if
    you prefer

To garnish
Mix together 2 tsp each ground
    pistachios and almonds and 1 tsp
    poppy seeds

Preparation 10 minutes | **Cooking** 10–15 minutes | **Serves** 4–6

Put 2 teaspoons of the tea in a saucepan over medium heat with about half of the measured water and bring to the boil. Boil until frothy then add the bicarbonate of soda and whisk vigorously for about 10 seconds. Add the remaining water and the crushed cardamom and boil until the tea broth becomes a bright red colour.

Reduce the heat to medium low and add the milk. Using a whisk, whisk the tea broth very vigorously to achieve a slight froth. The colour of the tea should now be dark pink. If you add more milk, the colour becomes even lighter.

Finally, add the salt or sugar and stir. Pour into a cup and sprinkle with the mixed crushed pistachios, almonds and poppy seeds.

Elaichi chai

Cardamom milky tea

The true chai of Pakistan, this slow-brewed milky tea should be made with loads of heady cardamom.

3 tsp Assam tea leaves
500ml/17 fl oz/2 cups water
5 green cardamom pods, crushed
500ml/17 fl oz/2 cups whole milk
4 tbsp caster (superfine) sugar
    (or to taste)

Preparation 10 minutes | **Cooking** 15 minutes | **Serves** 4–6

Put the tea, water and cardamom into a large saucepan and bring to the boil. When it comes to the boil, add the milk and return to the boil. Once that reaches the boil, reduce the heat to very low and simmer for 10 minutes.

Add the sugar and stir. Simmer for a further 5 minutes. Add more milk or sugar, if liked.

Pour through a sieve into a cup or glass and serve hot.

Rose milkshake

Children growing up in Pakistan were often promised a treat of rooh afza dooth – milk mixed with a rose, herb and spice syrup which can be bought in almost all Asian stores. You can use the store-bought syrup if you can find it, but homemade rose syrup makes a refreshing alternative.

For the rooh afza-style syrup (makes about 1 litre/1¾ pints/4 cups)
1 litre/1¾ pints/4 cups water
250g/9oz/1¼ cups caster
    (superfine) sugar
10g/⅓oz gum – Arabic gum,
    finely crushed then dissolved in hot
    water and cooled
½ tsp crushed aniseed
1cm/½-inch cinnamon stick
½ tsp crushed cardamom seeds
3–4 tsp rose water
2–4 drops red natural food colour

For the rooh afza-style milk
2–3 tbsp Rooh Afza-style syrup
250ml/9 fl oz/1 cup whole milk
1 tbsp basil seeds, soaked for
    15 minutes

Preparation 1 hour **Cooking** 5 minutes + cooling | **Serves** 8–10

To make the rooh afza-style syrup, bring the water with the sugar and add the dissolved gum, aniseed, cinnamon and cardamom to the boil in a saucepan, then turn off the heat. Add the rose water and food colour and allow to cool.

Strain the mixture through a sieve and pour into a sterilised bottle. Store in the fridge and use within 7 days.

To make the milk, add 3 tablespoons of the syrup with the milk into a blender and blend until frothy. Adjust the sweetness, if liked. Pour into a glass with ice cubes and top with soaked basil seeds.

Sindhi thadal
Almond milk, poppy seed and aniseed

Soothing for the soul and based on a classic Sindhi recipe, this nutty drink is made by soaking and grinding almonds to create a milk. It's then spiced with ground aniseed, poppy seeds and a hint of rose water.

150g/5½oz/1 cup blanched almonds, 500ml/17 fl oz/2 cups boiling water
50g/1¾ oz/¼ cup caster (superfine) sugar, or to taste
500–750ml/17–26 fl oz/2–3 cups water
1 litre/1¾ pints/4 cups ice-cold water
1 tbsp white poppy seeds
2 tsp aniseed, ground
1 tbsp dried edible rose petals, crushed by hand and sprinkled on top

Preparation 15 minutes + overnight soaking | **Cooking** 10 minutes | **Serves** 4

In a bowl, soak the almonds in the measured boiling water in the fridge overnight. The next day, blend the soaked almonds with their soaking water into a very fine paste.

Put the sugar with the 500–750ml/17–26 fl oz/2–3 cups water in a saucepan and heat gently over a low heat until the sugar has dissolved and a syrup has formed.

Combine the almond paste with the measured ice-cold water and the sugar syrup. Chill in the fridge for a few hours.

To serve, stir in the poppy seeds and crushed aniseed, sprinkle with rose petals, then pour over ice cubes.

Spiced sugarcane juice
With kalanamak and ginger

Summer in Pakistan sees stallholders bring out their sugarcane juice presses. The juice is freshly squeezed then laced with a kalanamak (black salt) and ginger for a kick – the perfect way to bring relief from the sun.

200ml/7 fl oz/scant 1 cup freshly squeezed sugarcane juice, or store-bought
½ tsp kalanamak (black salt)
1cm/½-inch piece ginger, peeled

Preparation 20 minutes | **Serves** 4

Blend all the ingredients together in a blender until frothy. Serve over ice cubes.

Nimbopani

Lemonade with salt and sugar

A simple combination of small yellow Pakistani lemons with sugar, salt and mint makes a refreshing drink that gently brings solace in a Pakistani summer. You can find these intensely citrusy lemons in Asian stores, but this can be made with any lemons.

Preparation 15 minutes | **Serves** 6–8

6 small South Asian lemons or 3 large lemons, squeezed
4–5 tbsp caster (superfine) sugar (or to taste)
1½ tsp sea salt
5 mint leaves, plus extra to garnish
lemon slices, to garnish

Blend all the ingredients except for the mint leaves in a blender until frothy.

Add the mint leaves and blend for 5 seconds. Serve over ice cubes garnished with mint leaves and lemon slices.

Cardamom and coconut mattha lassi

This is a typical Punjabi lassi which is made using full-cream, unhomogenised milk and full-cream yogurt – no water is added. I have added cardamom and used coconut yogurt. You could also just use plain Greek yogurt with desiccated coconut.

Preparation 10 minutes | **Serves** 2

250g/9oz/1 cup coconut whole milk yogurt (or use 250g/9oz/ 1 cup Greek yogurt with 2 tbsp desiccated/dry unsweetened coconut)
3 cardamom pods, seeds removed and finely crushed
200ml/7 fl oz/scant 1 cup whole unhomogenised milk
caster (superfine) sugar, to taste

Blend all the ingredients in a blender until very frothy, then serve over lots of ice cubes.

Salty lassi with cumin

Pakistani lassi is salty when paired with food, and sweet when drunk as a refresher between meals. The frothy topping comes from a lot of blending, which is traditionally done with a wooden hand whisk, but can be achieved with a blender. Using whole milk and yogurt works best.

Preparation 10 minutes | **Serves** 4–6

250g/9oz/1 cup whole set yogurt
25ml/1 fl oz/2 tbsp whole creamy unhomogenised milk
½ tsp salt
1 tsp caster (superfine) sugar
½ tsp dry-roasted cumin seeds

Blend all the ingredients, except the cumin, in a blender until frothy. Pour over ice cubes and garnish with the cumin. The addition of the cumin brings out the drink's saltiness.

Kanji
Mustard-fermented carrot and beetroot drink

This is a recipe that's made in northern Punjab and one that my aunts prepared with blood-red Pakistani carrots (which only grow in winter). No other carrots come close in colour or flavour, but if lacking these, I add beetroot, which gives the drink a similar redness as well as a lovely tang.

Preparation 15 minutes + 3–5 days fermenting | **Makes** About 2 litres/3½ pints/8 cups

5 carrots, cut into long 5cm/2-inch pieces
1 beetroot, peeled and cut into 4 pieces
juice of ½ lemon
2 litres/3½ pints/8 cups water
1 tsp red chilli powder
3 tbsp yellow mustard seeds, roughly ground in a mortar and pestle
1 tsp kalanamak (black salt)

Put the carrots, beetroot and the remaining ingredients into a large ceramic bowl or jar and cover with a lid or muslin cloth.

Place in a sunny or warm place for 3–5 days, stirring every day with a wooden spoon (not metallic, as it reacts with the pickling liquid) until mixed.

Taste each day and when it tastes sour, the kanji is fermented and is ready. Strain the fermented liquid and serve cool over ice cubes.

Any left over carrots and beetroot can be served as a delish relish.

Aam panna
Raw mango sharbat

You can freeze this sharbat in ice-cube trays – when you want a drink, pop a few cubes into a jug, add water to dilute and serve. Truly nothing else cools the body and calms the mind like a cold glass of aam panna.

3 raw green mangos
150g/5½oz/½ cup caster
  (superfine) sugar
1 tsp ground ginger
½ kalanamak (black salt)
1 tsp salt
250ml/9 fl oz/1 cup water

Preparation 30–40 minutes | **Serves** 8–10

Preheat the oven to 160°C/325°F/gas mark 3. Cover each raw mango with foil and place in the oven for about 25–30 minutes, or until the mangos are soft. Remove, allow to cool then peel off the skin and set the flesh aside.

Make a syrup with the sugar by adding 300ml/10 fl oz/1¼ cups water, or enough to cover the sugar in a saucepan and heating until the sugar melts.

Using your hands, squeeze the mango flesh into a bowl. Add all the spices and seasonings and mix together. Add the sugar syrup and stir. You can now either freeze all the mixture or use now.

To make the drink, add 1–2 tablespoons of the mixture to a blender with 2 ice cubes and the measured water and blend until frothy. Serve with more ice or add more of the mango mixture if you prefer. Adjust the seasoning to taste.

Spiced pomegranate sharbat

Sharbat is a sweet fresh juice, and this one is a particular favourite. It's made with freshly blended pomegranates with a touch of spice. You can make it ahead of time during pomegranate season and freeze. If you find it too strong when defrosted, add loads of ice to dilute.

2 pomegranates, shelled, juice
  squeezed and seeds discarded
½ tsp dried ginger
2 tsp dry-roasted ground cumin seeds
½ tsp salt
½ tsp chaat masala (see p26)
¼ tsp ground black pepper

Preparation 10 minutes | **Serves** 4–6

Blend all the ingredients in a blender until frothy then strain and pour over ice cubes to serve.

Summers under the tamarind tree
Spiced tamarind drink

After a day of picking fresh fruit from my Nani's (maternal grandmother) evergreen tamarind tree, I'd always be treated with this piquant drink – the ultimate remedy for tiredness. This drink alone is the best memory of the many childhood summers I spent lounging under her tamarind tree. Savouring each sip, I would sit on my Nani's breezy veranda, catching her distant chatter with my mother from the kitchen as they cooked. I never learned to cook by penning down recipes – it was during such moments when I unknowingly absorbed the sounds, sights and aromas of the food, made with passion and generosity in my home. It's those valuable lessons that bring to life the food that I know and love as Pakistani, and which I look forward to passing on to my daughter.

4 tbsp tamarind pulp (from 200g/7oz dried or fresh tamarind, see p23)
2 tbsp brown sugar
1 tsp kalanamak (black salt) or 1 tsp chaat masala (see p26)
500ml/17 fl oz/2 cups water
quartered thin slice of lemon
4 mint leaves, finely chopped

Preparation 15 minutes + 15 minutes soaking + 30 minutes chilling | **Serves** 4

Soak the tamarind pulp in a bowl of hot water for 15 minutes, then squeeze and strain. See more on how to get a good tamarind pulp on p23.

Blend all the ingredients, except the mint, in a blender, then chill in the fridge.

When ready to serve, stir and pour over lots of crushed ice. Add the lemon slice and sprinkle with chopped mint leaves.

Acknowledgements

Writing this book began with the simple belief in the authentic flavour of Pakistan. It has been a journey of remembrances and self-discovery. Though these are my words and recipes, none of this would have been possible without the help of many people, whose dedication, belief and support have made this book both a wonderful experience for me and a gift to those who read it.

I begin by thanking my supportive commissioning editor, Zena Alkayat, who has believed in *Summers Under the Tamarind Tree* from the moment she first read the proposal. Her hard work and that of her team has helped me make it a reality.

I would like to thank my friend, the food photographer Joanna Yee, who has captured the essence of the cuisine in each food picture. Working with her was a pleasure – her photography and keen eye for styling has made the book visually stunning.

I thank Shaukat Niazi, who has generously contributed many of the Pakistani location shots, giving this book visual authenticity and an insight into the food culture of Pakistan.

I give my gratitude to Madhur Jaffrey, who has offered such kind words in support of this book. She is someone I admire and have had the privilege of working with. Thank you to Olia Hercules and Meera Sodha for their lovely words about this book.

I will be forever indebted to my mother for being my teacher and my fiercest critic. Thank you for sharing so many of your recipes and secrets. And thank you to both my mother and father for being my eternal supporters. And my Nani and Dadi who are no longer: I thank you for being the inspiration behind this book.

Most importantly, I would like to thank Graeme Taylor. Without you this book would have always remained just a dream. Thank you for sacrificing your precious time to help me make sense of so much in this book and most of all sharing my dream. I couldn't have written this book without your support, patience and belief in me.

Finally a thank you to my daughter Ayaana Jamil, who has patiently watched her mama cooking, writing and generally being food obsessed, and for helping me roll those koftas and cut those tomatoes. May this book be your guide to your heritage as you grow.

Further thanks to…

Anne Faber, for pointing me in the right direction.
Claudia Young (Greene & Heaton), my agent, for always having supported my book.
Sarah Allberrey, for this beautiful book design.
Kathy Steer, for recipe editing.
Jamie Schler, for being a mentor from this book's inception.
Ceramica Blue, for the loan of some of the props on p156, p163, p168, p171.
Marilyn Williams and Patrick Fuller, for lending us their lovely garden for the Chai-pani chapter.
Ceri Jones, for the loan of her pretty hands on p156.

And a big thank you to friends and family who generously shared recipes, including my mother
Kausar Usmani, Moneeza Khan, Humaira Shaikh, Samina Ibrahim, Farida Sheikh, Tanveer Saleem,
Nuzhat Usmani and Anwar Yazdani.

It is not always possible to acknowledge each and every person involved, so a general thank you all
those who have made this book a reality. I hope that their efforts coupled with these stories and
recipes help you appreciate the passion, dedication and love of my cuisine and the hard work of the
many who make a cookbook possible.

For more about me and my work, please visit: sumayyausmani.com

Index